Praise for *How to Ex, Anything to Absolu*

Andy Tharby's *How to Explain Absolutely Anything* ...nyone tackles a fundamental aspect of teaching that has been take ᵣanted by far too many for far too long. The book not only enquires into explanation, but also ventures further and deeper – offering a wise and compelling exploration of curriculum, knowledge, memory, human psychology, and much more.

In age an of superficial media and bombastic TED Talks, Tharby brings evidence and intelligence to bear in order to reveal, in intricate detail, what makes for powerful teacher explanations. I'd happily recommend this book to absolutely every teacher.

**Alex Quigley, Senior Associate, Education Endowment Foundation
and author of *Closing the Vocabulary Gap***

In *Explain Absolutely Anything to Absolutely Anyone*, Andy Tharby skilfully explores the importance of high-quality explanation and offers teachers clear guidance on what they can do better in order to achieve it.

By starting with the significance of subject knowledge and teacher credibility, Andy opens up various frameworks for consideration before going on to suggest effective classroom strategies to put into practice. He has filled this practical, evidence-informed book with a range of clear illustrations and examples, and does not shy away from difficult questions surrounding teaching and learning.

Explain Absolutely Anything to Absolutely Anyone will be of great value to all teachers of all subjects.

**Dr Brian Marsh, Principal Lecturer in Science Education,
School of Education, University of Brighton**

In this excellent and beautifully written book, Andy Tharby addresses the topic of how teachers across all subjects of the curriculum can develop their capacity to explain with clarity, precision, flair and agility.

Rooted in research, Andy's captivating and persuasive arguments are bolstered by his practical experience and carefully considered reflections (as a learner as well as a teacher) as he explores the importance of subject knowledge and debates the key principles underpinning effective explanations. He then goes on to outline practical tips and guidance, helpfully punctuated with specific examples, for mastering the art yourself.

Andy cleverly presents his ideas by using the very strategies he suggests, helping us to understand the significance of clear and compelling explanation. And he does so in such a clear and compelling way!

Jill Berry, leadership consultant and former head teacher

How to Explain Absolutely Anything to Absolutely Anyone fills a considerable gap – as while the importance of explanation has long been recognised, nowhere has its role, application and impact been so clearly articulated as in this book.

In his beautifully crafted prose, Andy Tharby hones in on the significance of a teacher conveying the purpose of their subject and shares important ideas which will inform current conversations around the curriculum.

All great books provide new insights into old dilemmas, and *How to Explain Absolutely Anything to Absolutely Anyone* does exactly that. It is both scholarly and accessible, and should be essential reading for all involved in education. I shall be referring to it on a daily basis.

Mary Myatt, education adviser, writer and author of
Curriculum: Gallimaufry to Coherence

If you're like me, you may already think you are pretty deft at explaining tricky concepts with clarity, and even with a bit of panache. Upon reading this wonderful book, however, you realise that you still have a great deal more to learn about the science and craft of explanation, as Andy Tharby shares all there is to know on the subject.

Offering well-researched, practical guidance on how to plan and execute sharper explanations, *How to Explain Absolutely Anything to Absolutely Anyone* should be required reading for all teachers. A simply superb read.

Phil Stock, Deputy Head Teacher, Greenshaw High School

In *How to Explain Absolutely Anything to Absolutely Anyone*, Andy Tharby guides teachers to the point of peak performance: offering clear guidance on how they can boost the credibility of their subject knowledge in order to support pupils' long-term learning.

When it's done well, a curriculum can unlock a world of opportunity – for both the pupils and the teacher – but only when delivered by those teachers who bring the content to life. Tharby delves into what lies beneath the surface of subject knowledge and reveals a set of complicated building blocks, such as the use of modelling and the application of concrete examples, which combine to form great classroom teaching.

How to Explain Absolutely Anything to Absolutely Anyone arrives at the perfect time for the teaching profession and is full of super strategies to use in your own professional development.

Ross Morrison McGill @TeacherToolkit – the UK's most followed educator on Twitter, who writes at TeacherToolkit.co.uk

How to explain

absolutely anything to absolutely anyone

The Art & Science of Teacher Explanation

ANDY THARBY

Crown House Publishing Limited
www.crownhouse.co.uk

First published by
Crown House Publishing Limited
Crown Buildings, Bancyfelin, Carmarthen, Wales, SA33 5ND, UK
www.crownhouse.co.uk

and

Crown House Publishing Company LLC
PO Box 2223, Williston, VT 05495, USA
www.crownhousepublishing.com

British Library Cataloguing-in-Publication Data

A catalogue entry for this book is available from the British Library.

Print ISBN 978-178583367-0
Mobi ISBN 978-178583389-2
ePub ISBN 978-178583390-8
ePDF ISBN 978-178583391-5

LCCN 2018957152

Printed and bound in the UK by
TJ International, Padstow, Cornwall

To my son, George,
and to every other young person who just wants to know more.

Acknowledgements

This book is the result of many years of teaching, reading and conversation. I am especially grateful to Fran Haynes, Tod Brennan, Chris Runeckles and Shaun Allison, who have all, with humour and patience, taken the time over the last year to extend and question my thinking on a daily basis.

I thank everyone at Crown House for the meticulous effort you put in to every book you publish. I am so grateful that you agreed to publish this one. A huge thank you to my partner in crime Jason Ramasami whose illustrations create an energy and clarity that I could never achieve in plain words.

Thanks too to Mum and Dad for all the encouragement, not to mention all the school holiday babysitting that allowed me the time and space to write. And finally to Donna, who not only allowed me to break my promise that I would never write another book, but supported me unfailingly throughout the process.

Contents

Introduction

"Daddy, in football, is a striker the same as a forward?"

"Daddy, why do we have wars?"

"Daddy, what would happen if all books were made of bacon?"

From the age of about two, children develop the intellectual ability to ask *why* questions. It is a vital developmental milestone. Their burgeoning curiosity about the world and their increasing proficiency with language means that they become desperate to learn more. To quench their new-found thirst for knowledge and understanding, they seek answers from the adults in their lives; their parents and teachers. They are becoming aware of what they do not yet know, or have not yet imagined, and they go on a tireless hunt for the further information and elaboration that might lift the veil on the mysteries of the universe. George, my 6-year-old son, asked me the three questions above over the period of time I spent writing this book. (Be assured, this book *is* suitable for vegetarians!)

Nothing could be more natural to human language and communication than explanation. Explanations have a range of purposes: to make something understandable; to clarify and expand an idea; to give the causes, context and consequences of a situation or event; or to show how facts and concepts are related and connected. The most straightforward definition of an explanation is 'the answer to a question'. As members of language communities, we provide and receive countless explanations every day, at work and at play. This is why the word 'because' is one of the most important in the English lexicon. If the question is 'why', the explanation finds its origin in 'because'.

It is near impossible to conceive of effective teaching without explanation. A teacher who does not explain is little more than a mute babysitter. However, classroom explanations – also known as 'instructional explanations' – are more problematic than those that occur spontaneously in the course of ordinary life. This is because the recipients of the explanation, our students, have not previously sought out the new information that we require them to learn. Sometimes, they are not aware of what they do not know. More troublesomely, they sometimes hold misconceptions which mean that they are completely convinced of an alternative and inaccurate 'truth' to the one we hope they will learn. Sometimes the problem lies in a lack of motivation, especially when students fail to see the relevance of the new material that we are trying to explain.

It would seem sensible, then, to assume that if young people are to learn about the nuances of tectonic shift or the finer details of atomic structure, their teachers should learn how to explain these ideas with clarity, precision, flair and agility. It would also seem sensible that a sizeable portion of teacher training and development be dedicated to helping teachers to improve their ability to explain these concepts. Sadly, this could not be further from reality. In recent years, teacher talk – the most efficient form of explanation known to man – has become the black sheep of the education world. In some schools, teachers have been encouraged to talk less so that their students can talk more. Group-work and student-to-student discussion have become the gold standard, lauded and applauded despite their considerable limitations when students are working with new material. Teachers have been discouraged from speaking for too long, and in some cases have been hung, drawn and quartered for doing so!

Thankfully, the tables are beginning to turn. Common sense and research evidence are converging to reassert the importance of the teacher's role in the classroom and, more significantly, the importance of the things that the teacher has to say. In 2014, teacher and writer Daisy Christodoulou's *Seven Myths About Education* methodically dismantled many prominent misconceptions about teaching and learning. In response to those who argue that teacher-led instruction is passive, Christodoulou wrote:

> There is a reason why it took humans such a long time to discover the laws of nature, even though the evidence for such laws was all around them in the environment. We do not find it easy to learn new information when we have no or minimal guidance.[1]

Each new generation stands on the shoulders of the last. Few young people can understand the theories of Charles Darwin and Albert Einstein, or fully appreciate William Shakespeare and Mary Shelley, without guidance and explanation from an expert teacher. It is essential that teachers feel confident enough to stand up at the front and teach such world-changing content without the accusation of being didactic or overly dominating. There is a time for teachers to talk; and there is a time for students to listen. Of course, there is also a time when the reverse is more desirable and students should be working independently and autonomously. But this should usually happen towards the end of a sequence of learning, not at the beginning. In most cases, teachers should first provide answers and then open the space for interrogation.

A wealth of empirical evidence supports the assertion that teacher explanations perform a crucial role in learning. Educationalist John Hattie systematically analyses the effectiveness of different influences on learning. At the time of writing, his most recent list of 252 separate influences placed 'teacher clarity' at a very significant number 24.[2] John Hattie and Gregory Yates have also shown that teaching is

---

1 Daisy Christodoulou, *Seven Myths About Education* [Kindle edn] (Abingdon: Routledge, 2014), loc. 1033.
2 See Sebastian Waack, Hattie Ranking: 252 Influences and Effect Sizes Related to Student Achievement, *Visible Learning*. Available at: https://visible-learning.org/hattie-ranking-influences-effect-sizes-learning-achievement/.

much more effective when teachers use methods that *activate* learning rather than methods that *facilitate* learning.[3] Put simply, students usually learn better when a teacher introduces new content rather than attempts to elicit it from them. Moreover, evidence from cognitive science reveals that the less prior knowledge a student has about a topic, the more teacher guidance they need. Human cognitive architecture is simply not designed to learn difficult new concepts independently.[4] Further evidence points towards the constructive influence of face-to-face interaction between teacher and student. For instance, one study shows that students' learning and persistence outcomes are better when they take in-person courses than when they take online courses.[5]

Needless to say, not all teacher talk is effective talk. Too often, simple concepts are made too complex and complex concepts too simple. Students can be left uninterested or overwhelmed. We must also stay vigilant against a pair of familiar adversaries: decreasing attention and wandering minds. Even though verbal explanations are a staple component of almost every lesson, it is also well-established that they do not always work for all students.[6] However, this does not mean that teachers should limit their talk; it means instead that they should learn how to talk better. Explanations are to teaching what penicillin is to medical practice: essential but not effective in every case.

Research into effective teaching also reveals some fascinating and quite counterintuitive insights. In the US, Professor Siegfried Engelmann has compiled over half a century of evidence supporting Direct Instruction, a model of teaching that involves scripted explanations. Engelmann argues that what children learn is totally consistent with the input they receive from a teacher. Direct instruction involves precise clarity of wording, the use of carefully designed examples, and the teaching of rules and 'misrules' – all delivered through a systematic trickle of new information. Direct Instruction is a mastery approach to learning, which means that 85% of lesson time is devoted to practising material that children have

3   John Hattie and Gregory Yates, *Visible Learning and the Science of How We Learn* (Abingdon: Routledge, 2014), p. 73.
4   Paul A. Kirschner et al., Why Minimal Guidance During Instruction Does Not Work: An Analysis of the Failure of Constructivist, Discovery, Problem-Based, Experiential, and Inquiry-Based Teaching, *Educational Psychologist*, 41(2) (2006): 75–86.
5   Eric Bettinger and Susanna Loeb, Promises and Pitfalls of Online Education, *Evidence Speaks Reports* 2(15) (9 June 2017). Available at: https://www.brookings.edu/research/promises-and-pitfalls-of-online-education/.
6   See Jörg Wittwer and Alexander Renkl, Why Instructional Explanations Often Do Not Work: A Framework for Understanding the Effectiveness of Instructional Explanations, *Educational Psychologist* 43(1) (2008): 49–64.

already covered, while only 15% involves weaving in new material.[7] A nine-year longitudinal study called Project Follow Through found that students who received Direct Instruction had significantly higher academic achievement, better problem-solving skills and higher self-confidence and self-esteem than students receiving any other type of instruction.[8] Engelmann's slow and careful methods are a far cry from the rush and clamour of the way the curriculum is delivered in primary and secondary schools in England.

....

Before we start to explore the how, let's take a moment to think about what we might be trying to achieve each time we launch into an explanation. Chris Anderson, the curator of the non-profit organisation TED, gives this advice to would-be public speakers: "Your number-one mission as a speaker is to take something that matters deeply to you and to rebuild it inside the minds of your listeners."[9] This 'rebuilding' metaphor is essential to our understanding. The most effective explanations are designed and crafted with subtlety. As with the most robust physical structures, explanations should be built to last. The content we teach – whether it's quadratic equations or the respiratory system or dramatic irony – is not only for understanding and admiring now, but also for storing away for the future. A new fact, concept or idea is a gift for life, not a short-term loan.

There are many different types of instructional explanation. Teachers routinely explain facts, concepts, procedures, moral and aesthetic truths, metacognitive strategies and more. Each type of explanation comes with its own distinctive set of tricks and skills and a corresponding collection of hitches and hazards. We will explore these in full as we move through the book.

Explanation is an art form, albeit a slightly mysterious one. We know when we hear and see a teacher unravelling a great explanation. It has something to do with their effortless subject knowledge, the simplicity and directness of their language and the sense of assurance they exude. Nevertheless, we struggle to describe the intricacies of the craft. Just *how exactly* are they doing it? Invariably, we attribute good

7   See Shepard Barbash, *Clear Teaching: With Direct Instruction, Siegfried Engelmann Discovered a Better Way of Teaching* (Arlington, VA: Education Consumers Foundation, 2012).
8   See https://www.nifdi.org/what-is-di/project-follow-through.
9   Chris Anderson, *TED Talks: The Official TED Guide to Public Speaking* [Kindle edn] (New York: Houghton Mifflin Harcourt, 2016), loc. 262.

explanation to elements of a person's character or talents: "they're so confident" or "they explain things really clearly" or "they know their subject really well". However, these assumptions are unhelpful because they suggest that the ability to explain is a God-given gift; a form of tacit knowledge that some possess and others do not. In fact, explanation involves a set of intricate tools that anyone can master with a little patience and practice.

To unveil these hidden mysteries we will dip our toes into several forms of evidence. We will draw from educational research, from curriculum theory, from cognitive science, from the study of linguistics, from communication studies, from ancient philosophy and from the expertise of great teachers. We will look at how the most effective speakers, presenters and writers can transform even the most messy, complicated idea into a thing of wondrous crystalline clarity. And lastly, I will share some anecdotal accounts from my own English lessons of how I have attempted, often clumsily, to improve the way in which I explain new ideas in my classroom.

The idea of writing this book came to me on a rainy Saturday afternoon when I was halfway through the first chapter of Carlo Rovelli's *Seven Brief Lessons on Physics*.[10] I had wanted to read a book about physics for a while; it is a subject I know very

10 Carlo Rovelli, *Seven Brief Lessons on Physics*, Simon Carnell and Eric Segre (trs) (London: Penguin, 2015).

little about and one that has always somewhat intimidated me. I was struck immediately by the way in which Rovelli welcomed me into this new and potentially hostile world. Suddenly, the theory of relativity – for so long the impenetrable playground of wiry-haired science types – was something that even I, in my limited way, could begin to grasp. But more than that, it was lucid, strange and enticing. Beautiful even. I wanted to find out more.

How did Rovelli paint this new world so vividly? Let's begin with his bluntly put first sentence: "In his youth Albert Einstein spent a year loafing aimlessly."[11] Immediately, Rovelli opens a gap between expectation and reality by disrupting our conventional beliefs about Einstein: he seems more like a conventional teenager than a prodigious genius-in-waiting. Rovelli then plants us in a very specific time and place: Italy at the turn of the nineteenth century. Success stories are driven by obstacles that stand in the way of the protagonist's goal, and Albert's story as it progresses is no different: "his theory of relativity did not fit with what we know about gravity, namely how things fall".[12] In fact, Einstein had found himself – theoretically at least – pitted against a titanic foe: Isaac Newton, the godfather of Western physics.

After framing his narrative, Rovelli pops himself into the story. He recounts the moment on a sunny beach in Calabria where, in the pages of a mouse-gnawed book, he finally appreciated the magnitude of Einstein's theory. Looking up from the book and out to sea, Rovelli envisaged "the curvature of space and time"[13] as Einstein described it. This is an emotional and finely drawn epiphany – note the wonderful contrast between the tatty, nibbled book and the unimaginable greatness of the cosmos.

As he moves more deeply into scientific theory, Rovelli brings the mysteries of reality alive through metaphor. Space is described as a "gigantic flexible snail-shell", the earth as "a marble that rolls in a funnel". Other sentences are written with remarkable economy: "The gravitational field is not diffused through space; the gravitational field is that space itself".[14]

Rovelli's short chapter includes many of the tools vital to a great explanation: an interesting story; a clear context; an unsolved problem; a personal involvement; a

11 Rovelli, *Seven Brief Lessons on Physics*, p. 1.
12 Rovelli, *Seven Brief Lessons on Physics*, p. 2.
13 Rovelli, *Seven Brief Lessons on Physics*, p. 4.
14 Rovelli, *Seven Brief Lessons on Physics*, p. 6.

journey from the concrete to the abstract; the precise use of metaphor to capture hard-to-imagine concepts; and a vividness and economy of language. Teachers can certainly learn a lot about the art of explanation from reading books on complicated topics written for a lay audience, like Rovelli's.

Needless to say, skilful classroom explanation is about much more than word choice and the odd deft figure of speech. For example, students arrive in our classrooms with widely differing prior knowledge, which then influences how much they can comprehend and commit to memory. Furthermore, the language of many subjects, such as mathematics, goes far beyond spoken and written English. Images, diagrams, graphs and visual organisers are part and parcel of the symbolic code of learning. We should also be clear that explanations are *not* lectures. Ideally, they involve a dialogic process that involves active listening and participation from every person in the room.

A teacher's use of language also has a wider purpose: to induct students into the academic discourse of each subject. Think of each subject as having its own *grammar*; its own language world. This is a set of language conventions – involving phraseology, syntax, vocabulary and idiomatic expressions – that reflects the kind of thought processes inherent to the discipline and used with ease by subject experts. Consider the importance of conditional clauses – *if … then* clauses – to scientific thinking: *if* you freeze water, *then* it becomes a solid. Or the way in which English literature relies on tentative and exploratory language: the poet *seems to hint* that power dissipates and fades with time. Only students from academic families are likely to already be familiar with these language worlds. Unless we actively and purposefully model the implicit grammar of our subjects, we will struggle to improve our students' thinking, speaking or writing. Think of yourself as a member of an exclusive language club. How will you equip all your students to get past the bouncers on the door so they can join you inside? This task is even harder for primary teachers, whose role it is to induct students into multiple subjects and multiple language worlds.

Good teacher talk also improves students' vocabulary. This is particularly relevant at the time of writing as the new knowledge-rich primary and secondary curriculums in England require students to acquire an ever-deeper knowledge of words. Unfortunately, one in five children in England join secondary school unable to read to a standard that enables them to access the curriculum.[15] Of 24 OECD countries, England is the only one where 16–24-year-olds have lower literacy skills than 55–65-year-olds.[16] Knowledge of words and syntactical conventions (the arrangements of words and phrases in sentences) is not only vital to the development of reading competency, but also the key to unlocking academic success. A student will only build their vocabulary through regular and repeated exposure to new words, ideally through lots of reading. However, as only just over one-third of schoolchildren in England read at home every day, a teacher's deliberate and targeted use of words can go some way towards providing this exposure.[17]

In the chapters that follow, we will explore seven key principles for explanation that apply to every subject, age group and educational phase. These are:

Chapter 1: Subject knowledge

Your subject knowledge is both your magic bullet and your Achilles heel.

Chapter 2: Credibility and clarity

All explanation is also an act of persuasion.

Chapter 3: Explanation design

Too much new information at once can reduce learning. Less is usually more.

Chapter 4: Concepts, examples and misconceptions

Abstract concepts should be supported by concrete examples.

Chapter 5: Metaphor and analogy

Connections should be forged between students' prior knowledge and the material to be learnt.

Chapter 6: Storytelling

Your students are pre-wired to learn from storytelling.

---

15 Department for Education, *Reading: The Next Steps: Supporting Higher Standards in Schools.* Ref: DFE-00094-2015 (London: Department for Education, 2015). Available at: https://www.gov.uk/government/uploads/system/uploads/attachment_data/file/409409/Reading_the_next_steps.pdf, p. 13.

16 OECD, *Country Note: England and Northern Ireland (UK): Survey of Adult Skills First Results.* Available at: http://www.oecd.org/skills/piaac/Country%20note%20-%20United%20Kingdom.pdf, p. 4.

17 Liz Twist et al., *PIRLS 2011: Reading Achievement in England* (Slough: NFER, 2012). Available at: https://www.nfer.ac.uk/publications/PRTZ01/PRTZ01.pdf, p. 73.

Chapter 7: Elaboration

Explanations are only effective when students are also given the opportunity to think about the new material.

The conclusion explores ways in which you can hone and practise your explanations, and how to support other teachers in improving theirs.

Ultimately, the purpose of this book is to introduce and explain a series of concepts and processes that will help you to think differently about the way in which you introduce and explain new knowledge and skills. Each section also provides very simple and practical strategies that you can put into action straight away.

We will examine both the art and the science of explanation, and I will argue that to be most effective it requires a judicious blend of poetry and precision.

Let us begin.

Chapter 1
Subject knowledge

Your subject knowledge is both your magic bullet and your Achilles heel.

Picture the scene. It's 1995 and a GCSE German lesson is in full swing. Twenty or so slouching 15-year-olds chat away merrily around a motley collection of ramshackle tables. They are paying scant attention to the graffitied textbooks open on their desks – or to their teacher who is hopelessly beseeching them to speak *auf Deutsch*! As soon as the teacher's back is turned, a spotty lad grasps the leg of the chair of the boy sitting beside him. He gives it a quick jerk, and the chair's occupant sprawls to the floor. The boys at the table erupt into a wave of sniggers. Their beleaguered teacher erupts too – into rage at the boy floundering pathetically on the floor, not at his spotty assailant.

That was the sum of my learning about the GCSE German curriculum: how to get my peers into trouble as a result of my underhand behaviour. Needless to say, I failed my German GCSE and, needless to say, my memory of those lessons is now tinged with regret. The problem was that I did not value the subject of German. I was not motivated to try, and eventually sought validation through more nefarious means.

Any discussion about teacher explanation must start with the academic subject that is being taught, and any discussion about an academic subject must start with the justification of its value to those who are studying it. Broadly speaking, there are two types of value inherent in any school subject: its *instrumental value* and its *intrinsic value*.

The instrumental value of a subject is defined by the way in which its knowledge can be exchanged for future advantage; for the greater good of society or for the individual student. At a national level, mathematics knowledge benefits the financial and technological sectors, whereas employing individuals with knowledge of a second language allows British firms easier access to international markets. At an individual level, mathematics knowledge allows a person to run their own business or keep on top of their credit card bills, whereas knowledge of a second language allows access to niche job markets.

Over the past twenty-five years or so, education in England has increasingly been understood in this instrumentalist way: children go to school to enhance the long-term economic potential of the nation. In this vein, the quality of schools and teachers is now measured through exam results – those passports to the future – rather than by the quality of the curriculum or, by extension, the breadth and depth of what has actually been learnt. A simplistic rationale is in force: raise exam results and we create a skilled workforce who, in turn, will lead us towards greater economic prosperity and security in the future. Examination boards and Ofsted rule supreme in this brave new world where the boundaries between education's social purpose and its moral and philosophical aims have become blurred. Education is now expected to solve every problem in society – from social disadvantage to unemployment to the mental ill health of young people – and schools are scapegoated if they cannot provide this.

Intrinsic value, on the other hand, is the value we place in learning the subject for its own sake. Mathematicians, for instance, talk about the joy of being able to understand the world anew through symbolic notation. They describe the pleasure of solving a problem that once seemed impossible, or the beauty they find in logic and proof. Similarly, language teachers describe the value of learning a second language in terms of the way it introduces young people to a new culture, which then allows them to view the world through a new set of eyes and understand themselves and their own culture more distinctly. If only my teenage self had realised this!

Despite the current dominance of the instrumental model, we must not forget the intrinsic purpose of education: the *inherent* importance of our subject disciplines, their central ideas, concepts, questions and disagreements. This involves, of course, an appreciation of how education benefits and enriches individuals and society in ways that reach far beyond economic prosperity. The first role of explanation, I will argue, is the hardest of them all: to help children understand how subjects and subject matter are about much more than mere exam preparation. They are, instead, a valuable entryway to truth.

This cannot be achieved in a quick five-minute chat at the start of the year; this should infuse every lesson and every decision we make. We must communicate this message explicitly, of course, but also implicitly through our tireless championing of even the most thorny or mundane aspects of our subjects. Granted, we must also be pragmatic and clear-sighted about how far we can take our students; there is and always will be an instrumental reason for studying (and exam results do matter). But if we want students to find beauty, consolation or amazement in the curriculum – rather than emptiness and sterility – then we must start by explaining the aims and values that put our subjects on the map in the first place. Sure, the instrumental gains from studying a subject might allow you to dive deeply into your future; however, it is the intrinsic gains that give you the oxygen tank with which to breathe. Sadly, the current situation in English schools means the curriculum is being shrunk to the worst kind of reductionism, in which the subject has become indistinguishable from the exam.[1]

1   See Daisy Christodoulou's *Making Good Progress? The Future of Assessment for Learning* (Oxford: Oxford University Press, 2016) for a detailed discussion of this issue.

Consequently, there are two questions that each teacher must answer. First, what is the value of the subject (or subjects) I teach? Second, how will I help my students to understand and appreciate this value?

Consider the following prompts when thinking about how to make it clear that your subject is distinct, purposeful and interesting, especially in an opening lesson with a new class:

- **What's amazing about this subject?** Share two or three interesting examples or stories.

- **Why do I find this subject fascinating myself?** Personal disclosure builds trust.

- **Why do we study this subject in school?** Start with the intrinsic reasons before moving on to the instrumental.

- **What are the main debates and disputes within the discipline?** Explore a prominent, accessible example with the class and get them to decide where they stand on the issue.

- **What distinguishes this subject from others?** Explore the differences between your subject and two others.

- **How does a student do well in this subject?** Use an anecdote about a previous student.

- **How does a student do badly in this subject?** Use an anecdote about a previous student.

- **Where are we heading?** Tell the story of the curriculum as it will unfold over the coming year.

What is a subject discipline?

Some academic disciplines have their roots in ancient history (like physics) while others are relatively modern (like geography). Standish and Sehgal Cuthbert condense a wealth of curriculum theory into the following statement:

> Each discipline has its *own purpose, object of study, organizing concepts, modes of thought, conceptual framework of knowledge, and methods for validating and acquiring new knowledge.*[2]

Academic disciplines have been developed and defined by generations of scholars; they are social products, the combined work of people from the past and the present. In schools, these disciplines are redefined as subjects. School students rarely create new knowledge at the leading edge of the discipline; they are not ready for this quite yet. Instead, school subjects cover the early stages of learning and, as such, are much more about gaining a foothold in the discipline.

However, this does give us another insight into the role of explanation. The teacher's role is much more than to teach the knowledge and skills set out by the curriculum – the *micro-explanations*. It is also to induct the students into the subject discipline through its defining concepts and its modes of thinking; its traditions and its narrative. This is the *macro-explanation* of the subject that helps students to see how disciplinary knowledge develops and sheds light on human experience or natural phenomena. This interplay between the micro- and macro-explanations of a subject – the narrow angle and the wide angle – is one of the main themes of this book.

Here are some practical suggestions for embedding the subject discipline in lessons:

● Give subject-specific justifications of methods and processes: "In English we do it like this because …"

● Encourage students to think and speak in subject-specific ways: "How would a mathematician say this?"

2 Alex Standish and Alka Sehgal Cuthbert, Disciplinary Knowledge and School Subjects, in Alex Standish and Alka Sehgal Cuthbert (eds), *What Should Schools Teach? Disciplines, Subjects and the Pursuit of Truth* (London: UCL Institute of Education, 2017), pp. 1–19 at p. 8.

- Explain a word's meaning in the context of the subject: "I know the word 'factor' has different meanings in other subjects, but in maths it means ..."

- Pay special attention to the concepts and procedures that are essential to learning and mastering the subject: "This is a really important idea in history because ..."

- Make clear what must be memorised: "You must remember this idea in geography because it will help you with ..."

The shape and the journey

Is it possible to visualise the shape and structure of an academic subject? Sociolinguist Basil Bernstein thought it was. Bernstein theorised that academic discourses could be thought of as hierarchical or horizontal knowledge structures. Hierarchical subjects, such as the sciences, "create very general propositions and theories, which integrate knowledge at lower levels ..."[3] This idea of integration is key to the definition: new knowledge either refutes or is incorporated into existing theory. We can imagine hierarchical knowledge as a triangle with basic propositions at the base and more and more abstract ideas nearer the apex.

Other subjects have a horizontal structure. These subjects contain a series of "specialised languages with specialised modes of interrogation and specialised criteria for the construction and circulation of texts".[4] English literature, the social sciences and philosophy could be said to be horizontal subjects. The academic study of these is broken into separate 'languages' in the form of schools of criticism, modes of enquiry and discrete categories. Other horizontal subjects, such as mathematics, have separate modes of enquiry for separate problems – think algebra, trigonometry and geometry. Imagine horizontal subjects as being like a line that joins together each of these separate languages (L1, L2, L3, etc.) – as shown in the following illustration.

---

3   Basil Bernstein, Vertical and Horizontal Discourse: An Essay, *British Journal of Sociology of Education* 20(2) (1999): 157–173 at 162.
4   Bernstein, Vertical and Horizontal Discourse, 159.

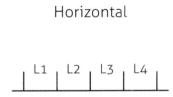

On a practical, day-to-day level I think it is wise to visualise each school subject as a combination of the hierarchical and the horizontal. Some subjects – for example, physics – are more hierarchical in form, and others – for example, English – are more horizontal. In addition, some subjects seek to describe natural phenomena or laws; others seek to develop moral or aesthetic judgement. Yet all are similar in the way in which they become more and more abstract as students progress through the years.

Perhaps it is more important for a school teacher to think about *how* learning progresses within the subject – what we need to learn first, what comes next, what comes after and so on. Christodoulou, in her discussion of effective assessment systems, refers to this as the 'model of progression'. This makes:

> **clear not just the starting point and the end goal but the steps along the way. These models of progression need to be specific to each subject because skills are specific, and do not transfer across subjects as easily as we might think.**[5]

If we combine Bernstein and Christodoulou's ideas, we reach the conclusion that each subject curriculum is unique in its shape and its long-term journey. There are many approaches to subject design, and there is no one way to create the perfect curriculum. However, it is vital that teachers work together to ensure that the curriculum we deliver has internal consistency and a clear rationale, so that it builds logically over a significant period of time. That way, we can communicate the story of our subjects with conviction. Our students need an explanation of why they are covering this topic now, how it connects to what they have done before and how it connects to what will come later. Similarly, they need to be shown how to find connections between and within topics and ideas. You can only do this by making

5   Christodoulou, *Making Good Progress?*, p. 212.

your subject's hidden, interconnecting 'tube map' distinct and visible to your students.

What should we be teaching?

Once we have some idea of the shape of the subject, we should turn our attention to the content we will teach – the raw ingredients. In England, the curriculum at Key Stage 4 is dominated by GCSE exam syllabuses and, in state schools at other key stages, by the requirements of the national curriculum. Despite the weighty influence of these, there is still much room for richness, depth and diversity in the curriculum.

In *Knowledge and the Future School* Michael Young describes the purpose of schooling in all phases:

> **It is to enable all students to acquire knowledge that takes them beyond their experience. It is knowledge which many will not have access to at home, among their friends, or in the communities in which they live.[6]**

He goes on to describe this knowledge as the 'right' of all students, whatever their personal circumstances. Young also argues that children should be taught what he calls 'powerful knowledge'. There are three features to powerful knowledge: it is

6   Michael Young, Knowledge, Curriculum and the Future School, in Michael Young, David Lambert, Carolyn Roberts and Michael Roberts (eds), *Knowledge and the Future School: Curriculum and Social Justice* (London: Bloomsbury, 2014), pp. 9–40 at p. 10.

different from the knowledge we pick up through everyday experience; it is organised into a set of related concepts and taught through subjects; and it is developed by specialists in the field – from geographers to novelists to economists.[7]

Consider this everyday scenario:

Emma, a 16-year-old girl, is walking through a town centre on a bright, cold winter Saturday. The streets are thronged with shoppers looking for bargains in the sales. On a bench sits a homeless man and his dog; the man is begging for change.

A deep and broad education rich in 'powerful knowledge' will give Emma some excellent tools with which to explain this everyday scene. In geography, she has learnt about weather systems and so she understands that the bright, cold day is the result of the way in which a high pressure system allows the air to cool and descend. In economics, she has learnt about the concept of supply and demand and so she understands why many shops have reduced their prices in January. In English, she has been reading George Orwell's *Down and Out in Paris and London* and she feels a pang of pity when she sees the homeless man and his dog – an echo of the feeling she had in class when reading about the destitute people in these 1920s cities. Emma's education has allowed her to see the wonder and sorrow of her surroundings in kaleidoscopic colour. She has constructed an intellectual hinterland that allows her to think and feel differently about the world.

This, then, must be the true aim of teacher explanation: to help students learn powerful knowledge – its facts, concepts and procedures – so that they can see the world in bright, discriminating detail. This comes with a proviso: powerful knowledge is not easy to learn. It requires the patience, resilience and hard work of the learner *and* the teacher. The skill of explanation, therefore, lies in finding ways to help Emma connect her existing knowledge of the everyday world to the organised, specialised and abstract knowledge of the academic world. We will explore this in more detail in Chapter 4.

---

7   Michael Young, Powerful Knowledge as a Curriculum Principle, in Michael Young, David Lambert, Carolyn Roberts and Michael Roberts (eds), *Knowledge and the Future School: Curriculum and Social Justice* (London: Bloomsbury, 2014), pp. 65–88 at pp. 74–75.

Subject knowledge is not enough

An extensive report from the Sutton Trust, entitled *What Makes Great Teaching?*, includes a useful summary of research into what is known as 'pedagogical content knowledge'.[8] This is defined by a teacher's understanding of how to adapt teaching approaches to fit the specific needs of the subject content.

This isn't purely knowledge of the subject, or purely knowledge of how to teach; it is an infusion of the two – rather like mixing red and blue to make purple. The report reveals that:[9]

- Studies have shown a relationship between teachers' content knowledge and learning gains made by their students.

- As yet, there is little evidence to suggest that a teacher's general ability or academic qualifications have an impact on their students' performance.

- Studies into middle school science teachers have shown that there is a positive but modest relationship between teachers' subject knowledge and students' learning gains.

- Support for teachers on the specific areas in which their subject knowledge and knowledge of common student misconceptions is weakest is likely to improve students' learning.

- Studies of maths teachers have demonstrated that a positive difference in a teacher's pedagogical content knowledge is associated with more than a month's additional learning for students in a year.

All in all, the little evidence we have suggests that what matters most is teachers' subject knowledge *and* their understanding of the ways in which students will think about the subject matter at hand. Therefore, we should bear in mind that having an encyclopaedic knowledge of your subject is not always enough; just as important is having an encyclopaedic knowledge of the nitty-gritty of the content to be taught and the difficulty students are likely to have with learning that content.

....

8   Robert Coe et al., *What Makes Great Teaching? Review of the Underpinning Research* (London: Sutton Trust, 2014). Available at: http://www.suttontrust.com/wp-content/uploads/2014/10/What-makes-great-teaching-FINAL-4.11.14.pdf.
9   Coe et al., *What Makes Great Teaching?*, pp. 18–20.

Shulman defined pedagogical content knowledge like so:

> I include, for the most regularly taught topics in one's subject area, the most useful forms of representation of those ideas, the most powerful analogies, illustrations, examples, explanations, and demonstrations – in a word, the ways of representing and formulating the subject that make it comprehensible to others.[10]

Pedagogical content knowledge, therefore, includes the ability to represent your content in multiple verbal and non-verbal ways. Becoming knowledgeable about your subject, then, should never be your sole objective. You need to develop your knowledge about how to teach your subject too.

The flip side of knowledge

In the introduction, I asserted that your subject knowledge is your magic bullet and your Achilles heel. Without excellent subject knowledge a teacher will always be limited in how far they can extend their students; however, good subject knowledge has an insidious side effect known as the 'curse of knowledge'. Put simply, this is the difficulty we have in imagining ourselves in the shoes of someone who does not know what we know. The term derives from economics and the finding that better-informed people find it very difficult to think about a problem from the perspective of less-informed people.[11] You have probably experienced this phenomenon when playing charades at Christmastime. No amount of miming a take-off and bashing your hands against the wall seems to work. To you, it seems exasperatingly obvious that the answer is *Chitty Chitty Bang Bang* – but not to your bemused family who stare at your lurching body movements in increasing bewilderment!

---

10 Lee S. Shulman, Those Who Understand: Knowledge Growth in Teaching, *Educational Researcher* 15(2) (1986): 4–14 at 9.
11 See Colin Camerer et al., The Curse of Knowledge in Economic Settings: An Experimental Analysis, *Journal of Political Economy* 97(5) (1989): 1232–1254. Available at: https://www.cmu.edu/dietrich/sds/docs/loewenstein/CurseknowledgeEconSet.pdf.

Steven Pinker ascertains that the curse of knowledge:

> is far more than a curiosity in economic theory. The inability to set aside something that you know but that someone else does not know is such a pervasive affliction of the human mind that psychologists keep discovering related versions of it and giving it new names.[12]

The problem is that when we know something very well we forget the stages that we had to go through to learn it in the first place. It's hard to see how something that we find so easy might be impossible to somebody else. Coupled with this is the likelihood that when you were a schoolchild you enjoyed and found success in the subject you now teach. This makes it even tougher for you to imagine what the experience of learning your subject is like for an unmotivated or unskilled member of your class.

Nobody can hold a lens to a human mind to see what it sees. What appears concrete and crystal clear to you, might feel abstract, misshapen and missing key information to another.

---

12 Steven Pinker, *The Sense of Style: The Thinking Person's Guide to Writing in the 21st Century* (London: Penguin, 2014), p. 59.

To some extent the curse of knowledge is unavoidable. Nevertheless, here are six tips to help you to mitigate the effect of the curse of knowledge in your classroom:

● **Punctuate your explanations with examples.** The more you use the phrases 'for example', 'for instance', 'it's like' and 'such as', the easier students will find it to keep up with you when you are explaining abstract ideas. See Chapter 4 for more ideas.

● **Add a few words of explanation after any technical term or difficult piece of vocabulary.** For example, "This play represents the apogee – *the highest point* – of Shakespeare's career."

● **Keep another example up your sleeve.** "OK, I can see some of you are still unsure. Try thinking of it this way ..."

● **Teach through opposites.** "Remember it was x, *not* y, that caused ..."

● **Find out what they really know and think.** Sometimes we leave lessons thinking things like "They really liked it when I did x" or "They really got y when I explained it like that." Often, however, we have not thoroughly sampled the class. If we only question and listen to the brightest and keenest students – i.e. those who put their hands up more often than others – then we are likely to assume that all students share this enthusiasm and understanding. This, unfortunately, perpetuates the curse of knowledge.

● **Take the temperature of the room regularly.** Keep your eyes peeled for multiple turned heads or subtle cues that students are struggling to understand. Often these cues are very slight. Sometimes children will adopt crafty strategies to trick you and their peers into thinking that they understand. Let your instinct be your guide.

Developing subject knowledge

There are known knowns; there are things we know that we know. We also know there are known unknowns; that is to say, we know there are some things we do not know. But there are also unknown unknowns; the ones we don't know we don't know.[13]

Donald Rumsfeld was the US secretary of defense in George W. Bush's administration. You have just read his infamous explanation of US scepticism about the development of weapons of mass destruction by Iraq, which preceded the outbreak of the Iraq War in 2003. Even though Rumsfeld's comments were lampooned in the media at the time, his amateur philosophising about 'known knowns', 'known unknowns' and 'unknown unknowns' offers a useful way of thinking about subject knowledge:

- **Known knowns.** These are the aspects of subjects and topics that we are most confident in and, it is likely, we can explain most clearly. However, be careful not to be too confident about your own academic knowledge and qualifications. Studies have shown, for instance, that pre-service science teachers, even those with a good degree, often possess basic misconceptions about chemical ideas.[14]

- **Known unknowns.** These are the areas of the curriculum in which we are aware of our knowledge gaps. As long as we plan to fill them – through reading, training or working with experienced colleagues – they do not necessarily present a problem.

- **Unknown unknowns.** These lurk beneath the surface in sinister silence. Maybe you don't realise that you don't fully understand how to solve an exponential equation. Maybe you don't understand how to read *Frankenstein* through the lens of feminist theory, even though the teacher in the classroom next door is doing it with aplomb. Perhaps you haven't yet got to

13 Donald Rumsfeld, the then US secretary of defense in a 2002 departmental briefing about Iraq's weapons of mass destruction. See: https://www.youtube.com/watch?v=GiPe1OiKQuk.
14 Vanessa Kind and Per Morten Kind, Beginning to Teach Chemistry: How Personal and Academic Characteristics of Pre-Service Science Teachers Compare with Their Understandings of Basic Chemical Ideas, *International Journal of Science Education* 33(15) (2011): 2123–2158.

grips with the misconceptions students have about the differences between socialism and capitalism. When we couple this with what psychologists call the 'overconfidence effect' – the fact that we, as human beings, systematically overestimate our knowledge and skill in almost every domain – then we have a problem. It is likely that we are not quite as good at explaining things as we think we are.[15]

What we need, therefore, is a set of tools or methods that enable us to discover more about our subject knowledge limitations, the effectiveness of our explanations and the areas we need to improve. Ideally, this would involve a whole-school approach to subject-specific professional development. In reality, many schools in England are not yet providing this opportunity to their staff, preferring generic forms of continuing professional development (CPD) instead. The advice below is separated into advice for individual teachers, department leaders and school leaders.

Advice for teachers

To gain a greater insight into the depth of our own knowledge, we need to compare it to someone else's. To do this we can regularly observe other teachers in our department. Even better is to observe or contact a teacher in another school, because groupthink – when bad decisions are made by a group because its members do not want to express opinions that others may disagree with – is a very real problem among people who have worked together for a long time. This is an area in which Twitter has filled an important gap. My favourite strategy, however, is reading. The more we read books, blogs, journals and articles about our subject, the more we can fill the remaining gaps and add to the intricate finery of our subject expertise.

15 See this blog post for an interesting discussion of the overconfidence effect: Rolf Dobelli, The Overconfidence Effect: Why You Systematically Overestimate Your Knowledge and Abilities, *Psychology Today* [blog] (11 June 2013). Available at: https://www.psychologytoday.com/blog/the-art-thinking-clearly/201306/the-overconfidence-effect.

Advice for department leaders

Too often department meetings can become all about administration rather than CPD. You could ring-fence some time in each meeting to discuss an aspect of subject knowledge. There are a host of ways in which this could be done. In a maths departmental meeting, a teacher who is especially good at teaching higher level coordinates could model how they do this to the rest of the department. In an English departmental meeting, a teacher who has read a recent biography of Shakespeare might be given ten minutes to share insights from the book that would be useful in helping Year 11s' understanding of the cultural context of *Macbeth*.

Advice for school leaders

A 2015 review of international research into teacher professional development found that subject-specific CPD is more effective than generic pedagogic CPD, in terms of its impact on pupil outcomes.[16] The report from the Teacher Development Trust suggests that effective CPD should be underpinned by:

● Subject knowledge.

● Subject-specific pedagogy.

● Clarity around learner progression, starting points and next steps.

● Content and activities dedicated to helping teachers understand how pupils learn, both generally and in specific subject areas.[17]

A more recent report into current practice suggests that even though subject-specific CPD is favoured by teachers *and* appears to have more impact on pupil outcomes, schools in England, especially those struggling in terms of pupil outcomes and inspection results, lag behind other high-performing countries in delivering high-quality subject-specific CPD.[18]

16 Teacher Development Trust, *Developing Great Teaching: Lessons from the International Reviews into Effective Professional Development* (London: Teacher Development Trust, 2015). Available at: http://TDTrust.org/about/dgt.

17 Teacher Development Trust, *Developing Great Teaching*, p. 20.

18 Philippa Cordingley et al., *Developing Great Subject Teaching: Rapid Evidence Review of Subject-Specific Continuing Professional Development in the UK* (Coventry: CUREE, 2018). Available at: http://www.curee.co.uk/node/5032.

There are some wonderful exceptions, however, that provide a potential solution. At Durrington High School in West Sussex, where I teach, departments meet on a fortnightly basis to improve their pedagogical content knowledge. The meetings focus on two questions:

1   What are we going to teach in the next two weeks?

2   How will we teach it well?

To end the chapter, a great example comes from the science department at Durrington who were about to teach Year 10 how to use moles to find the ratio of reactants and products, and how to balance symbolic equations. This is quite a challenging topic, especially if you are not a chemistry specialist.

The session went like this:

Steph Temple, the head of science, modelled on the whiteboard how she goes through the process of solving these equations, just as she does when she is teaching the class – stressing the importance of starting from the basics to make sure they are secure and then working up. Every step of the process was discussed and unpicked. Staff felt comfortable to ask questions such as "Why did you do that bit like that?" or to offer their own input.

As she went along, she pointed out the common mistakes that students make and how to avoid them.

She also pointed out some challenges to add in, especially when going through the basics – e.g. adding in some $(OH)_2$ when working out the relative formula mass.

With a particularly tricky question, a mistake was made which actually proved to be a good discussion point for the team. What do they need to stress in their explanation/modelling to ensure that their students don't make similar mistakes?

The team were then given the opportunity to try out lots of similar problems for themselves, while discussing the possible sticking points with each question and how they would overcome them.[19]

19 For more see: Shaun Allison, Now That's What I Call CPD, *Class Teaching* [blog] (24 April 2017). Available at: https://classteaching.wordpress.com/2017/04/24/now-thats-what-i-call-cpd/.

Chapter summary

- Each subject has its own story and tradition. We should explain it in terms of the intrinsic value of learning the subject, the shape and organisation of the subject, and the way learning progresses in the subject.

- The aim of explanation is to introduce students to powerful knowledge that exists outside of their everyday experience. This is the entitlement of every student.

- There are three areas to work on to improve our subject knowledge which will, in turn, improve the effectiveness of our explanations. These are: improving our understanding of the common misconceptions that students have when learning the subject; improving our understanding of where and when we might be vulnerable to the 'curse of knowledge'; and identifying and improving the 'unknown unknown' gaps in our subject knowledge.

First steps

- In no more than fifty words, write down what you believe to be the intrinsic value of your subject.

- Go online and order yourself a book on an area of subject knowledge in which you feel least confident.

- Email your subject leader or school leadership team to try to persuade them to embrace the concept of subject-specific CPD. Point them in the direction of the two reports we have touched upon in this chapter: the Teacher Development Trust's *Developing Great Teaching* and Cordingley et al.'s *Developing Great Subject Teaching*.

Chapter 2
Credibility and clarity

All explanation is also an act of persuasion.

The legendary nineteenth-century novelist Charles Dickens was hugely critical of the Victorian education system. In 1854, Dickens channelled his disaffection into a monstrous caricature who epitomised the 'factory model' of schooling that he so despised. This was the schoolmaster Thomas Gradgrind, from *Hard Times*, whose cold insistence on factual learning served to strip his pupils of their basic individuality and humanity:

Thomas Gradgrind, sir – peremptorily Thomas – Thomas Gradgrind. With a rule and a pair of scales, and the multiplication table always in his pocket, sir, ready to weigh and measure any parcel of human nature, and tell you exactly what it comes to. It is a mere question of figures, a case of simple arithmetic. You might hope to get some other nonsensical belief into the head of George Gradgrind, or Augustus Gradgrind, or John Gradgrind, or Joseph Gradgrind (all supposititious, non-existent persons), but into the head of Thomas Gradgrind – no, sir!

In such terms Mr. Gradgrind always mentally introduced himself, whether to his private circle of acquaintance, or to the public in general. In such terms, no doubt, substituting the words 'boys and girls,' for 'sir,' Thomas Gradgrind now presented Thomas Gradgrind to the little pitchers before him, who were to be filled so full of facts.

Indeed, as he eagerly sparkled at them from the cellarage before mentioned, he seemed a kind of cannon loaded to the muzzle with facts, and prepared to blow them clean out of the regions of childhood at one discharge. He seemed a galvanizing apparatus, too, charged with a grim mechanical substitute for the tender young imaginations that were to be stormed away.

'Girl number twenty,' said Mr. Gradgrind, squarely pointing with his square forefinger, 'I don't know that girl. Who is that girl?'[1]

Gradgrind is a teacher who is armed with knowledge; a teacher who will stop at nothing to fill the 'tender' minds of his pupils with useless and disassociated facts. There is no art or discovery in his classroom. Oh no, for Gradgrind, the world of knowledge is simple and geometric, bleached of any introspection or beauty. Here is a teacher whose relationship with children is hard and purely functional, so much so that he knows his students as numbers rather than as people.

1   Charles Dickens, *Hard Times* [Project Gutenberg ebook edition] (London: Chapman & Hall, 1905 [1854]). Available at: https://www.gutenberg.org/files/786/786-h/786-h.htm.

Even now, Gradgrind is a byword for someone who is obsessed with facts. Nevertheless, we should take Dickens' depiction of Gradgrind with a pinch of salt. The last thirty years of research into how the mind thinks and learns has shown that factual knowledge is vital to learning: it supports critical thinking, aids reading comprehension and speeds up learning.[2] The problem with Gradgrind is not so much his insistence on factual knowledge but the way in which he goes about instilling it in his students. We know intuitively that Gradgrind is a terrible teacher. He speaks only to the head and not to the heart.

In the previous chapter we looked at the knowledge of the teacher. This chapter will begin to examine the *character* of the teacher. All human communication relies on an exchange of information between people – in the form of thoughts, ideas or feelings. For effective classroom explanation, the relationship between communicator and receiver – the teacher and the student – really matters. The notion of credibility – the quality of being convincing and trustworthy – is central to this relationship and is the focus of the first part this chapter. In the second half, we will move on to explore *teacher clarity*, an essential aspect of credibility and a necessary prerequisite for learning.

Ethos, logos, pathos

As well as being persuaded to appreciate the intrinsic worth of the material they are studying, young people also need to buy into the value of effort and persistence, especially when the work is difficult or feels purposeless (as, inevitably, it sometimes does during the early stages of learning). For this to happen, they must learn to trust us as their teachers. Ultimately, *all explanation is also an act of persuasion.*

We are helped by the work of the ancient Greek philosopher Aristotle, whose theories about rhetoric – the art of persuasion – have influenced public speakers for millennia since. Aristotle believed that there are three pillars (or *appeals*) of rhetoric: *ethos*, *logos* and *pathos*.[3] These are the ways in which a speaker can appeal to

---

2   Daniel T. Willingham, How Knowledge Helps: It Speeds and Strengthens Reading Comprehension, Learning – and Thinking, *American Educator* 30(1) (2006): 30–37. Available at: https://www.aft.org/periodical/american-educator/spring-2006/how-knowledge-helps.
3   Aristotle, *The Art of Rhetoric*, Hugh Lawson-Tancred (trs) (London: Penguin Classics, 1991).

their audience that form the backbone of spoken persuasion. Admittedly, pedagogy and rhetoric are separate arts and should not be confused. A class dynamic is far more complex, interpersonal and long-lasting than the fleeting relationship between a captivating orator and an enraptured audience. Nevertheless, Aristotle's ideas do point to the ways in which a teacher can sow the seeds of credibility, especially in the opening weeks of the academic year. As we know, first impressions count.

Ethos is the way in which we establish our credibility and build a connection with our audience. Logos is the way in which we influence others through reason and logic. And pathos is the way in which we provoke and anticipate the emotions of our audience.[4]

Here's an example:

Ethos: "Hi. I'm Barack Obama. Please make me a cup of tea."

Logos: "Hi. We are both thirsty and the only thing we have in the cupboard is a box of teabags. Please make me a cup of tea."

Pathos: "I am clasping an unloved puppy that has been left alone on the freezing streets of the city. If I put him down now, he will freeze to death. Please make me a cup of tea."

In practice, the three appeals are inseparable; they are interlinked channels of communication that can be applied in the classroom in myriad ways. The greatest teachers seem to magically combine all three, possessing: the ability to earn the trust of others; a wonderful depth of subject knowledge; and an acute understanding of how school makes young people feel.

Mercifully, rhetoric is not only an art, it is a skill that can be learnt. How, then, might the three appeals help us to better establish ourselves with our classes?

---

4   See Sam Leith's *You Talkin' to Me? Rhetoric from Aristotle to Obama* (London: Profile Books, 2012) for an excellent introduction to rhetoric.

Ethos

Our students need to know that we are trustworthy and fair, and that we have absolute faith in their ability to learn. Crucially, this must extend to all members of the group, even the hardest to reach.

We might do this by keeping our calm and playing any student misdemeanours with a very straight bat. We might model our love of our subject by explaining why it still fascinates us as fully grown adults. We might tell our classes that even though they are in Year 7, we will treat them like, and give them the work of, Year 10s. We might set challenging tasks right from the get-go or we might theatrically tear up a list of target grades, reminding them that they are human beings not numbers and projections. We hold no preconceptions and we expect the very best from each and every one of them.

Ultimately, successful teachers nurture two forms of authority. They are authorities of their subjects and authority figures in the eyes of their students.

Logos

It goes without saying that you cannot prove your ethos as a teacher without showing a considerable degree of logos. Reason and logic, of course, lie at the heart of most subject disciplines.

To activate the logos appeal, we could start the academic year by teaching a topic we know intricately, explaining it with clarity and detail and probing student thinking with agile questioning. We could use our planning time to add extra depth and texture to our subject knowledge, rather than frittering it away on unnecessary bells-and-whistles slide shows. We could also make it clear – in as kindly a manner as possible – that unexplained answers and incomplete reasoning will always be gently challenged between these four walls.

Pathos

Pathos is more than pity and empathy. It is about appealing to the full gamut of emotions – from excitement and fear to amusement and curiosity. Like logos, it has a huge influence on our ethos appeal and, in turn, on our credibility in the eyes of our students. However, the pathos appeal can be misapplied. We are never aiming to be our students' best friends.

A classroom can be a raging sea of emotion, particularly in a secondary school, and we must navigate it as best we can. First off, we should unearth the inherent emotion of our subjects in our delivery. We should consider carefully how we push children to achieve more without damaging their sense of self-worth. We should laugh together and we should question together. We should show that, yes, we too are human by being frank about our weaknesses. We should continue to remember that childhood is complex and that home lives can be difficult, yet we should never let this dent our expectations of any child.

Teacher credibility today

Aristotle's ideas are as relevant today as they were over 2,000 years ago. In fact, over forty years of rich and diverse research into the construct of 'teacher credibility' and its relationship with learning has taken place in the US. Eminent education researcher John Hattie's analysis places teacher credibility as number 12 of 252 of the most powerful predictors of student learning.[5] In characteristically blunt fashion, Hattie asserts that, "If a teacher is not perceived as credible, the students just turn off."[6] Put another way, if you exude credibility, your students are more likely to absorb your explanation. Unsurprisingly, there seems to be a strong relationship between the perceptions that students have of a teacher's credibility and the amount they learn from that teacher.

---

5   The *Visible Learning* blog lists them here: https://visible-learning.org/hattie-ranking-influences-effect-sizes-learning-achievement/.
6   Quoted in Darren Evans, Make Them Believe in You: Teacher Credibility is Vital to Learning, an Updated Study Reveals. But What Can You Do to Win Your Pupils Round?, *TES* (17 February 2012). Available at: https://www.tes.com/news/tes-archive/tes-publication/make-them-believe-you-0.

Nothing is ever that simple though. Once you start to delve into the research, you realise that the construct of credibility has a number of overlapping dimensions, and researchers have not always pinned down an agreed definition. However, a 2009 meta-analysis – a study that combines the results of multiple research projects – centred on a trio of underpinning principles: *competence, trustworthiness* and *caring*.[7]

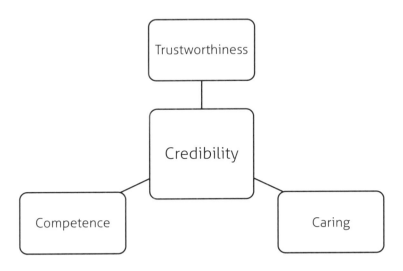

7   Amber N. Finn et al., A Meta-Analytical Review of Teacher Credibility and Its Associations with Teacher Behaviors and Student Outcomes, *Communication Education* 58(4) (2009): 516–537.

Competence

In the eyes of our students, our knowledge is vital; however, a teacher's perceived competence involves much more than this. Competence hinges on our ability to command and communicate our knowledge effectively. We can do this by planning and presenting our lessons in an organised and detailed way, and by supporting our delivery with relevant evidence and arguments. Research also suggests that teachers who make fewer grammar, enunciation and pronunciation mistakes are perceived as being more competent. Even sharing personal experiences and stories – including any success we have had personally in the field of study – can improve our students' perception of our competence.[8]

Trustworthiness

Trust is about placing your confidence in another. The trust a student gains for their teacher is earned through the process of teaching itself. Trust is fragile and can be ephemeral – hard-won but easily shattered. To gain a student's trust, you should aim for sincerity and honesty in your presentation and demonstrate how you apportion scepticism or trust. This might involve identifying issues of reliability and bias inherent within the subject material. Perhaps you might say: "While this source is interesting we should be careful not to fully trust it because …" Trust has also been shown to be a reciprocal process: the more trust we give students in the learning process, the more likely we are to earn it back.[9]

Caring

An essential ingredient of credibility is the goodwill we demonstrate towards our students. Caring is related to both competence and trust. Teachers who use caring messages – both verbal and non-verbal – are considered as competent and trustworthy by their students.[10] Try using sentence starters such as, "This topic is

8   William A. Haskins, Ethos and Pedagogical Communication: Suggestions for Enhancing Credibility in the Classroom, *Current Issues in Education* 3(4) (2000): 1–6.
9   Haskins, Ethos and Pedagogical Communication.
10 Jason J. Teven, Teacher Caring and Classroom Behavior: Relationships with Student Affect and Perceptions of Teacher Competence and Trustworthiness, *Communication Quarterly* 55(4) (2007): 433–450.

important to me because …" or "I'm really interested in what you think about …" or "You should care about this because …"

Conversely, teachers who are seen as incompetent – or even offensive! – are those who deliver confusing or boring lectures, exhibit a lack of knowledge, give too much or too little information, deviate too far from the syllabus or use an inappropriate volume; either too loud or too quiet.[11] Crucially, however, care should not be condescending or overbearing; instead it should provide a comfortable balance between support and challenge.

The essential point is this: show that you care about the content you are explaining and the people you are explaining it to. If you do, your students will come to see you as a credible teacher and, in turn, they will be more likely to learn from your lessons. As with trust, care is a give-and-take process. If you care, they care.

The authentic teacher

Should teachers behave as robotic clones or should we show fidelity to our true selves? In 2017, Zac D. Johnson and Sarah LaBelle conducted a fascinating study into the concept of teacher authenticity. They asked 297 US college students to describe the behaviour of authentic and inauthentic teachers. From the results, they concluded:

> **authentic teaching is perceived when teachers are viewed as approachable, passionate, attentive, capable, and knowledgeable. Alternatively inauthentic teaching is observed when teachers are perceived as unapproachable, lacking passion, inattentive, incapable, and disrespectful.[12]**

This study presents an illuminating insight into how students perceive their teachers. For instance, students find teaching authentic when teachers tell personal stories related to the topic, share moments from their own education and empathise with the stresses and strains of being a student. Put simply, when we take off

11 Teven, Teacher Caring and Classroom Behavior.
12 Zac D. Johnson and Sara LaBelle, An Examination of Teacher Authenticity in the College Classroom, *Communication Education* 66(4) (2017): 423–439 at 423.

the cloak of professionalism to reveal our true humanity, our students genuinely appreciate it. Interestingly, many students respond well to teachers who seem to be speaking from their own thoughts rather than repeating from a textbook. That is not to say that textbooks should be avoided, just that the teacher's role is to add texture and life to their material. Beware, too, of simply reading directly from your slide show. Your students may well deem you 'incapable' if you do not add meaningful contributions of your own.[13]

Authentic teaching is not about pretending to be someone you are not. Nor is it advisable to fill your lessons with a warts-and-all account of your private life. Instead, Johnson and LaBelle's study suggests that there are two keys to authenticity: recognise your students as individual people and be yourself. However, we should remain conscious that studies like this only give us an indication of how students think about their teachers; they do not necessarily tell us what kind of teacher attributes lead to better learning outcomes for students.

Your knowledge is appealing

Even though the research into teacher credibility and teacher authenticity is very useful, its insights should be applied with kid gloves. We will not improve our effectiveness as teachers by working on our appeal alone. This would be akin to filling your kitchen with top-of-the-range cooking equipment but ignoring the need to buy ingredients for your recipe! In fact, the research we've reviewed so far is conclusive in its finding that our credibility and authenticity are the result of our mastery over the subject content we are teaching. Nevertheless, we can all enhance the effectiveness of our explanations by ensuring that our comments and actions exhibit trust, care, competence and authenticity.

Finally, it is important to note that the research findings outlined in this chapter are based on correlations, which means that a reverse or alternative causal relationship could also be contributing to the effect. In other words, successful students might be more likely than their unsuccessful peers to rate their teachers as credible. We should also note that most of these findings derive from studies on US college students, rather than children in UK schools.

....

13 Johnson and LaBelle, An Examination of Teacher Authenticity.

While these studies provide some universal insights, we should remember that a child's perception of their teacher is always influenced by context. A very credible primary school teacher, for example, would become decidedly unconvincing if they attempted to teach a class of 16-year-olds in the way they would 6-year-olds! Similarly, the credible maths teacher may have a very different teaching style to the credible English teacher. Credibility, therefore, is always dependent on situation and setting.

Teaching with clarity

The education world overspills with thrilling sounding initiatives – from 'flipped classrooms' to one-to-one tablets; from forest learning to discovery-based learning. Each new innovation is jumped upon eagerly by hoards of school leaders and education consultants keen to try on the emperor's new clothes. Yet one of the most powerful influences on learning is so simple and unfashionable that it is often overlooked: a teacher's capacity to explain things clearly.

A pertinent example of the powerful effect of clear teaching comes from the Wabash National Study, a large-scale, longitudinal project that took place between 2006 and 2012, and set out to investigate the conditions and experiences that influence the outcomes of liberal arts education in the US.[14] Over 17,000 participants from forty-nine colleges took part, and the results were quite a surprise, even to the researchers.

Even though many diverse and innovative teaching practices – such as academic challenge, undergraduate research and active learning – were shown to have a promising effect:

> a set of questions that focused on the seemingly more mundane practice of clear and organized instruction had as much – or more – impact on student growth than many of the other, more innovative good and high-impact practices.[15]

14 See http://www.liberalarts.wabash.edu/study-overview/.
15 Charles Blaich et al., Instructional Clarity and Organization: It's Not New or Fancy, But It Matters, *Change: The Magazine of Higher Learning* 48(4) (2016): 6–13 at 8.

The clarity and organisation of teaching was shown to have a significant positive relationship with nine major learning outcomes including 'academic motivation', 'critical thinking', 'interest in engaging in intellectually challenging work' and even 'psychological wellbeing'.[16]

In the study, the clarity and organisation of instruction was measured by asking students how often they had experienced ten separate features during their time studying at college. These included:

● "Faculty gave clear explanations."

● "Faculty made good use of examples and illustrations to explain difficult points."

● "Faculty effectively reviewed and summarized the material."

● "Faculty interpreted abstract ideas and theories clearly."[17]

The fascinating – and counterintuitive – thing about these findings is that very straightforward teacher-led approaches appear to lead to rich, diverse and progressive outcomes. You do not need to flip your classroom or funnel your maths curriculum through the medium of thrash metal to motivate, inspire, engage and support your students. Instead you should consider what those bells and whistles are really adding – otherwise they might just be extraneous noise.

Nevertheless, we should maintain some degree of scepticism about findings like these. It could also be the case that measurements of teacher clarity are influenced by a student's cognitive ability or level of motivation. For instance, some individual students may be able to find clarity and meaning in the most lacklustre and disorganised of teacher explanations; however, it is likely that most will not.

---

16 Blaich et al., Instructional Clarity and Organization, 8.
17 Blaich et al., Instructional Clarity and Organization, 8.

Clarity in the classroom

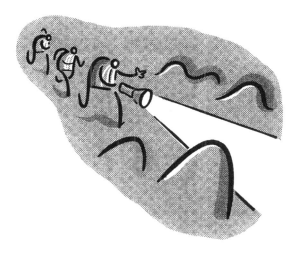

So what exactly does clear teaching look like? Ironically, this is where things start to become a little murky. The combined results of nearly 200 separate studies have demonstrated that teacher clarity has a moderate effect on student cognitive learning.[18] Yet despite the evidence that clarity is a constituent of effective teaching, there is remarkably little description of the features of clear teaching in these studies.

We can begin to unravel the mystery by looking at Dylan Wiliam's work on effective formative assessment. Wiliam has whittled his advice down to five key strategies. The first, and most crucial, is "clarifying, sharing, and understanding learning intentions and criteria for success".[19] In English schools, this suggestion is sometimes misinterpreted as meaning that every lesson needs a learning objective. This represents a crude simplification of Wiliam's work. In truth, genuine clarity should permeate every part of the teaching process, not just the opening

18 Scott Titsworth et al., Two Meta-Analyses Exploring the Relationship between Teacher Clarity and Student Learning, *Communication Education* 64(4) (2015): 385–418.
19 Dylan Wiliam, *Embedded Formative Assessment* [Kindle edn] (Bloomington, IN: Solution Tree Press, 2011), loc. 1015.

moments of a lesson. Imagine, for example, that you are about to teach a physics lesson with the objective "define and understand the terms 'mass defect' and 'binding energy'". That's a completely clear objective. However, your students will only learn something if you explain and model mass defect and binding energy with great lucidity, and if you provide precise and comprehensible feedback along the way.

It is not enough merely to proclaim your learning intentions clearly; you need to be clear at all points of the lesson. In the same way that the morning sun gradually illuminates the hills, the fields and the valleys from the east, clear teaching involves the incremental lighting up of each and every nook and cranny of the subject content itself.

Here are my six top tips for becoming a clearer teacher:

1. Share the rationale and identify your 'through-line'

Always explain how each lesson, or lesson section, fits into the long-term journey. What did we do before? Why are we doing this now? Where will we go next? Some teachers find a visual representation of the journey – such as a timeline – to be very useful.

Your through-line is the key concept or idea that you want students to take away from the lesson. In English literature, the through-line could be the idea that the novel you are reading is a vehicle for the writer's left-wing political beliefs. In drama, your through-line might be the concept of proxemics, which concerns the distance between characters and props on a stage and what this reveals about their relationships. Keep returning to these through-lines at various points in the lesson. These repetitions should not take the form of a single soundbite. Ideally, the through-line should be rephrased and reworded in subtle variations through-out the lesson – by you in the opening parts, and by your students as it progresses. This way, the essential concept comes to the fore, rather than the choice of words used to describe it. Nevertheless, memorable soundbites can be useful mnemonics to support long-term retention.

2. Use concise and concrete learning objectives

A lot of hogwash does the rounds regarding the correct wording of learning objectives. Often this leads to abstract, overcomplicated or awkward grammatical constructions. For example:

Students will be able to understand the way in which the poet uses metaphor and symbolism to explore the way in which time is both ephemeral and eternal and will be able to use analytical language to express their own ideas in a conceptualised and originally constructed format.

Eh? In schools that encourage such practice it is likely that students experience learning objectives as little more than pre-lesson white noise. I suggest you choose from two options: a title using as few words as possible or a question. For example:

- *The theme of time in 'Ozymandias'.*
- *How does Shelley explore the theme of time in 'Ozymandias'?*

Concise objectives, such as these, create a clear entry point to the lesson. They provide a simple catalyst for discussion and elaboration.

3. Use examples to set the standard

Multifaceted tasks like extended essay writing or portrait drawing require the application of a complex range of knowledge and skills. The final products are then assessed according to their relative quality and aesthetic appeal. However, it is very hard to put these abstract notions into words. "Paint a *beautiful* portrait" and "write an *insightful* essay" do not quite cut the mustard because the notion of quality relies on a subjective impression. Words cannot quite capture its true essence.

Instead, the most useful approach, where possible, is to set the standard with examples of work rather than with written statements. Presenting the class with a well-argued essay or a well-executed portrait will provide more clarity than written or verbal assessment criteria. It is a wise move to also point out the active ingredients of these examples. What makes this essay fizz? What causes this portrait to pop?

4. Couch success criteria in measurable, everyday language

Success criteria are useful because they provide a clear guide about what to include in a piece of work. However, the most misguided teaching advice I ever received was, "Give them the marking criteria to follow." This is a sure-fire way to reduce the clarity of your teaching. Exam board assessment rubrics are designed as tools for trained examiners; their purpose is not to guide learning, but to guide fair and accurate marking. In many subjects, assessment descriptors are saturated in vague language. What's the difference, for instance, between an 'insightful' or an 'evaluative' essay?

Instead, our success criteria should, where possible, be written in the imperative and couched in measurable, everyday language. Therefore, the assessment statement:

All points are fully explored in depth and detail.

... becomes a clear direction towards success:

Include at least four sentences in every paragraph so that all points are explored in depth and detail.

---

5. Accompany written feedback with concrete examples (or avoid it altogether if you can)

Written feedback works like Chinese whispers. Before correcting a mistake or writing a comment, we must first create a mental model – an act of the imagination in itself – of what was going through the student's mind at the time they made the error: i.e. what was the misconception or what knowledge was lacking? Then we must write a clear and concise comment to address this. Next, the student must read the comment and make their own mental model of what we were thinking when we wrote the comment – a further act of the imagination. Finally, the student must act upon this feedback in a way that leads to an improvement in their learning.

It is no wonder that less-adept learners gain so little from written feedback! If you struggled to understand a new concept in the first instance, it is unlikely that a couple of sentences of teacher feedback will rectify the issue. Four simple ways to improve the clarity of feedback are:

1 Find as many opportunities for verbal dialogue as possible. It is far easier to form a model of someone's thinking when you can ask them a question or respond immediately.

2 Once again, use examples and models to set the standard. Show a successful example – perhaps the most proficient in the class – and get students to edit and improve their work by comparing it to the example.

3 Identify the main areas students need to work on by quickly scanning through their work. Then provide detailed whole-class feedback on these.

4 Reteach. As detailed explanations and examples are not possible in written feedback, this is usually the most sensible option.

6. Create a knowledge organiser for each topic

A knowledge organiser is a simple tool that provides clarity for both teachers and students. Many students struggle to organise their subject knowledge into a useful format. A knowledge organiser solves this problem by arranging the most important and useful facts about a topic on a single page. For instance, in the characters section of my knowledge organiser on J. B. Priestley's *An Inspector Calls*, I have included:

Arthur Birling	1. pompous
	2. driven by reputation
	3. stubborn
	4. a social climber
	5. an archetypal capitalist
	6. ridiculed by Priestley
	7. middle class
	8. a caricature
	9. a misogynist
Sybil Birling	1. cold
	2. upper class by birth
	3. prejudiced
	4. infantilises her children
	5. no moral/social epiphany
	6. no remorse
	7. no transformation
	8. antithesis of her daughter
Sheila Birling	1. naïve (at the start)
	2. stereotypical middle-class young woman (at the start)
	3. becomes compassionate, perceptive and wiser
	4. a proto-feminist
	5. has a social and moral epiphany
	6. transforms
	7. use as a symbol of hope

These central points, numbered for greater precision, provide a solid framework around which students can construct and connect their deepening knowledge and understanding. The chief beauty of the knowledge organiser is that it allows for incredible clarity. Students know what they need to learn and retain, and teachers know what they need to teach.

Making the classroom code explicit

The final aspect of teacher clarity we shall explore involves making explicit the hidden language code – the privileged discourse – of the classroom. In the section below, English teacher Fran Haynes shares an overview of the theory and research that underpins 'code switching', along with practical strategies you can use in your classroom.

The problem

Teachers often work in contexts where there are tangible social disparities between groups of students, and between teachers and students. These differences commonly manifest themselves in classroom talk. For example, in one class, we might encounter the seemingly compliant student who does not cause any disruption, but also shrinks away from any attempt to engage with classroom talk, even a familiar exercise such as answering a question posed by their teacher. Next, we might find the student who has a strong vocal presence, but prefers to continue the banter of breaktime rather than switch to a more appropriate mode for the classroom. Finally, and perhaps most frustratingly, we might have the enthusiastic and perceptive student, who contributes insightful ideas during class discussion but then seems to hit a ceiling when faced with exam-style tasks on the exact same topics.

It is not surprising that these students are the ones most likely to underachieve and, more starkly, are often the ones who come from low-income homes. Thus, it seems apparent that there is a need to think more deeply about the social and cognitive role of language in classroom learning.

The research evidence

James Paul Gee defines discourses as "social practices" that involve "words, actions, values and beliefs" with which "members of a particular social group" adopt and perform an identity.[20] Speakers are apprenticed in early life to a primary discourse through scaffolded support from masters, usually their families. Subsequently, speakers are also apprenticed into secondary discourses as part of their socialisation, for example in schools.

Some discourses are more privileged than others as they confer control of social goods such as money or cultural authority, and thus bestow users with elevated status in society. The secondary discourse used in schools is an apt example of a privileged discourse in this sense. Significantly, the privileged secondary discourse used in schools is assimilated into the primary discourse of particular children, traditionally white and middle class, who are introduced at home to culturally specific ways of doing things, such as talking.

These children, therefore, encounter less conflict with the dominant discourse at school compared to children from homes where this discourse has not been introduced. Consequently, there occurs an inequality in the classroom: some children have to master a new discourse at the same time as learning the content of the lesson, whereas some children are able to dedicate their cognitive effort to the lesson content alone.[21]

Practical ideas for the classroom

Ultimately, it is the teacher's responsibility to level the playing field by ensuring that all students are inducted into the secondary discourse that we use daily in school. This can be tackled by making the rules and workings of the discourse

----

20 James Paul Gee, *The Social Mind: Language, Ideology and Social Practice* (New York: Greenwood Publishing Group, 1992), p. 107.
21 See James Paul Gee, *An Introduction to Discourse Analysis: Theory and Method* (Abingdon: Routledge, 2011) for a more detailed discussion.

explicit through modelling and scaffolding. Here are some suggestions for how this can be achieved in the classroom:

1. Scaffold the discourse

- *Share and practice ground rules for talk. For example, take turns to speak, justify your idea with opinions, seek other people's ideas, etc.*

- *Provide sentence stems for talk at pair, group and whole-class level. For example, "What do you think about ...?" and "I can see your point, but I disagree because ..."*

2. Model the discourse

- *Demonstrate how to use the ground rules and sentence stems with another adult or appropriate student in front of the whole class.*

- *Make the rules of the discourse visible before using it with the class. For example, "I am going to ask you some questions about ... because it will help me to identify ..."*

3. Expect students to engage with the discourse

- *Provide feedback on the discourse as well as on the lesson content. For example, "You've understood the poet's intention, but now give me your answer again using a tentative phrase, such as 'it may be the case ...'"*

Chapter summary

- By working on your pathos and logos appeals at the start of the academic year, you can avoid becoming a Gradgrind and develop your ethos as a credible and effective teacher.

- Your students will find you credible if they perceive you as competent, trustworthy and caring. And remember to be yourself!

- Students are likely to learn more if you organise and explain subject material very clearly. Ensure that learning objectives and success criteria are shared with utmost clarity. Use examples and knowledge organisers to set the standard whenever you can. Don't forget to model and scaffold the academic discourse of the classroom.

First steps

- Use the first two to three weeks of the academic year to stealthily establish your ethos appeal. Start by ensuring that you know the first topic you will teach inside out and back to front.

- Start using the phrases "I trust ..." and "I care ..."

- Design a knowledge organiser for the next unit you are to teach. If you can, work with a team of other teachers to boil down the active ingredients of the topic.

Chapter 3
Explanation design

Too much new information at once can reduce learning. Less is usually more.

How much should I tell my class and how much should they work out for themselves? This question cuts to the core of teaching. In recent years, teacher-led pedagogy – the sage on the stage – has become synonymous with didacticism, control and the over-exercise of adult power. Indeed, some schools are so concerned about adult domination of lessons that bizarre and arbitrary expectations have been crystallised into policy – for example, teachers are required to talk for no longer than ten minutes a lesson. The fear is that excessive teacher talk leads to passivity, lack of engagement and, crucially, a reduction in learning.

Sadly, the modern expectation of reduced teacher direction has hampered the potential of many capable new teachers and has distorted our shared professional understanding of what makes for effective teaching. In many situations, it is simply illogical to expect a child to discover something they do not know without being told it in the first place. Let's take a simple example. You need your Year 7 geography class to understand the concept of 'infrastructure'. You have three options: the first is to tell them what the word means using relatable examples; the second is to ask the class what they think it might mean in the hope that somebody already knows; the third is to put on a series of activities that will help the students to guess or discover the meaning on their own. It is obvious that the first option here is more coherent and efficient than the other two and will almost always lead to a more accurate understanding for those who have not encountered the word before.

Why unguided teaching is usually ineffective

In 2012, Paul A. Kirschner, John Sweller and Richard E. Clark wrote an influential article in which they explored the evidence showing that explicit teaching is usually more effective than minimal guidance.[1]

The dispute between advocates of minimal guidance and advocates of explicit instructional guidance has rumbled on for more than half a century. Explicit instructional guidance occurs when teachers "fully explain the concepts and skills that students are required to learn".[2] This guidance might take the form of teacher explanation, a lecture, a video, a computer presentation or a live demonstration. The information is explicitly taught and practised until support and structures are gradually faded out. At this point, problems and tasks can be solved and completed independently.

Meanwhile, minimal guidance approaches require students to "discover or construct some or all of the essential information for themselves".[3] This method has been given various names over the decades – including discovery-based learning, problem-based learning, inquiry learning and constructivist learning – and often involves situations where students attempt to mimic the behaviour of experts. For example, students in science lessons might try to discover fundamental scientific principles for themselves through investigations and experiments.

....

1   Paul A. Kirschner et al., Putting Students on the Path to Learning: The Case for Fully Guided Instruction, *American Educator* (spring 2012): 6–11.
2   Kirschner et al., Putting Students on the Path to Learning, 6.
3   Kirschner et al., Putting Students on the Path to Learning, 6.

The article concludes that:

> The past half century of empirical research has provided overwhelming and unambiguous evidence that, for everyone but experts, partial guidance during instruction is significantly less effective and efficient than full guidance.[4]

Worryingly, the minimal guidance approaches often recommended in English schools as examples of best practice are likely to:

- Favour the brightest and best prepared in the class.
- Lead to frustration for those who do not 'get it'.
- Encourage disengaged or confused students to copy their peers.
- Lead to misconceptions becoming entrenched.
- Take more lesson time than explicit approaches.
- Increase the achievement gap between more-skilled and less-skilled learners.

Advocates for minimal guidance often hypothesise that these approaches lead to students being better able to transfer their learning to new contexts. These claims, however, are not supported by evidence. Worryingly, studies also suggest that less-skilled students often prefer minimal guidance approaches – even though they are likely to learn less from them![5] Perhaps this is because they require less attention and concentration than listening to a teacher and following clear instructions.

There is, however, a caveat to these findings: the 'expertise reversal effect'. The more a learner knows about a topic, the less effective explicit guidance becomes. Experts, it turns out, do better with less guidance, whereas novices need much more. Kalyuga et al. state that:

> The most important instructional implication of this effect is that, to be efficient, instructional design should be tailored to the level of experience of

---

4   Kirschner et al., Putting Students on the Path to Learning, 11.
5   Richard E. Clark, Antagonism between Achievement and Enjoyment in ATI Studies, *Educational Psychologist* 17(2) (1982): 92–101.

intended learners. Without such tailoring, the effectiveness of instructional designs is likely to be random.[6]

Similarly, we should be aware of what psychologists call the 'generation effect': the fact that we are more likely to remember information when we have taken part in producing it than when we have received it from an external source such as a textbook or teacher explanation.[7] At first this might seem to contradict the argument for explicit instruction; however, on closer inspection it does not. Children cannot conjure up an advanced mathematical theorem or make a subtle critique of the theory of evolution by magic; only experts at the leading edge of their discipline can do this. The generation effect reminds us that when children have a good basis of foundational knowledge of a topic, they should be given tasks and questions that allow them to think, speak and write about the topic using their own words to generate their own ideas.

In truth, all primary age and most secondary age students would be classed as novice learners rather than experts. Still, we should be wary of a blanket, one-size-fits-all approach to teaching. A simple working principle might be that *the more they know about this topic, the less I need to tell them.* Be careful, however, not to misapply this rule of thumb. Quick learners will learn very little if they are subjected to years and years of minimal guidance. If they are to make genuine progress, these students need explanation to move them on to more advanced and difficult concepts instead. Higher attaining students, therefore, should never be left out to graze.

Long-term memory and working memory

Why are explicit teaching methods so effective? We must begin by examining the two central components of human cognition: the *long-term memory* and the *working memory*. In recent years, scientists have discovered that long-term memory is the dominant structure of human thought. We can envisage our long-term memory as a warehouse or hard drive which stores our knowledge of the world. Everything we know, or think we know, is stored here: from the aroma of freshly baked bread

---

6   Slava Kalyuga et al., The Expertise Reversal Effect, *Educational Psychologist* 38(1) (2003): 23–31 at 29.
7   See Robert Bjork's work on this here: https://bjorklab.psych.ucla.edu/research/#generation.

to cherished memories from our own schooldays; from how to drive a car to the meaning of the words you are reading in this sentence – all are stored in the long-term memory. And the long-term memory is not lazy or inactive: when students are working on a task – be it reading a poem, solving a maths problem or throwing a ball – they are mainly relying on the representations of these experiences in their long-term memories. We might not be conscious of its presence, but the long-term memory is always alert and ready to lend a hand. Daniel Willingham puts it perfectly: "Understanding is memory in disguise."[8]

The working memory, however, is much more limited. Here, very small amounts of information are stored for a very limited duration. If the long-term memory represents the human mental hard drive, the working memory represents the extremely inefficient human mental processor – the thoughts that are temporarily active. We use our working memory for language comprehension, problem-solving and planning. We can only hold on to a limited number of items at once – between three and five for young adults depending on the difficulty of the task – and there are differences in capacity between individual people.[9] Gathercole and Packiam Alloway note the stark differences that can occur in the average class:

> in a typical class of 30 children aged 7 to 8 years, we would expect at least three of them to have the working memory capacities of the average 4-year-old child and three others to have the capacities of the average 11-year-old child, which is quite close to adult levels.[10]

The problem is that working memory capacity can easily become overloaded, meaning that new information is not transferred to long-term memory. Working memory capacity difference, therefore, is one of the main reasons why some students learn more than others given the same teacher input. It explains why too much new information at once can reduce learning; *less is usually more*.

The wonderful thing about long-term memory is that it works independently of working memory; memories can be brought back to mind when they are needed.

8   Daniel T. Willingham, *Why Don't Students Like School? A Cognitive Scientist Answers Questions About How the Mind Works and What It Means for the Classroom* (San Francisco, CA: Jossey-Bass, 2009), p. 92.

9   Nelson Cowan, The Magical Mystery Four: How is Working Memory Capacity Limited, and Why?, *Current Directions in Psychological Science* 19(1) (2010): 51–57.

10 Susan E. Gathercole and Tracy Packiam Alloway, *Understanding Working Memory: A Classroom Guide* (London: Harcourt Assessment, 2007), p. 7. Available at: https://www.mrc-cbu.cam.ac.uk/wp-content/uploads/2013/01/WM-classroom-guide.pdf.

If a child knows their times tables, they can use this knowledge to solve more complex problems without placing any extra stress on the working memory. Similarly, if a child can read fluently – i.e. they can recognise complete words and sentence syntax automatically – then they can use their working memory to help with the more taxing task of comprehending the text being read. In much the same way as NHS, CIA and BBC are easier to remember that SHN, ACI and CCB, we chunk our learning into units or 'elements'. The more developed and fluent are students' mental schemas – the vast repositories of facts, concepts and procedures stored and organised in the long-term memory – the easier it is for them to learn new information. The long-term memory steps in to help out and thereby reduces the strain on the working memory.

Teacher explanations, therefore, have two important roles to play. First, they should be designed to ensure that they do not overload working memory. Second, they should help students to transfer new facts, concepts and procedures from working memory to long-term memory. In many ways, what we understand as 'learning' is really 'encoding in long-term memory'. Explanations must be carefully balanced. If they are too challenging then students are likely to experience cognitive overload, which leads to little learning. If they are not challenging enough, then they will lead to little productive thinking and, in turn, less encoding in long-term memory. The ideas in this chapter will help you to ensure that you get this balance just right.

Cognitive load theory

Cognitive load theory has developed from the work of Australian educational psychologist John Sweller's work on problem-solving. It is based on understanding the types of information held in working memory at any one time. These are known as 'intrinsic load', 'extraneous load' and 'germane load' and, added together, make up the capacity of the working memory.[11] Cognitive overload occurs when the capacity of the working memory is exceeded.

---

11 Centre for Education Statistics and Evaluation, *Cognitive Load Theory: Research That Teachers Really Need to Understand* (September) (Sydney: NSW Department of Education, 2017). Available at: https://www.cese.nsw.gov.au//images/stories/PDF/cognitive-load-theory-VR_AA3.pdf.

intrinsic load + extraneous load + germane load = total cognitive load

Intrinsic load

This is related to the difficulty of the subject matter being learnt. It is influenced by how complex the material is and by how much a student already knows about it. For example, 2 + 2 + 5 has less intrinsic load than 93 x 543, whereas understanding the workings of the human respiratory system has more intrinsic load than knowing where the lungs are situated in the human body.

Intrinsic load is also associated with prior knowledge. 2 + 2 + 5, for instance, is likely to have a high intrinsic load for a 4-year-old, whereas 93 x 543 might have a low intrinsic load for a mental arithmetic whizz. In general, higher intrinsic load is a feature of learning materials that contain 'high element interactivity'. This occurs when something can only be learnt by understanding many separate elements simultaneously, as is the case with learning about the human respiratory system.[12] It is important to recognise that intrinsic load is fixed and unchangeable – although as we will see later, there are some nifty ways of helping to reduce its influence.

Extraneous load

Extraneous load is bad for learning because it can hinder the construction of long-term memories. Unlike intrinsic load, extraneous load is related to how the subject material is presented rather than its inherent difficulty and, as instructional designers, we can either heighten or reduce its effect. If you have ever had a ridiculously over-packaged delivery – a DVD in a box that would fit a fifty-inch television, for instance – then you already have some notion of the redundancy of extraneous cognitive load. It is any extra and unnecessary thinking that students have to do that does not contribute to learning. We will explore how to reduce the extraneous load in your explanations in a moment. For now, remember that a

---

12 John Sweller, Cognitive Load Theory, Learning Difficulty and Instructional Design, *Learning and Instruction* 4 (1994): 293–312. Available at: http://coral.ufsm.br/tielletcab/Apostilas/cognitive_load_theory_sweller.pdf.

mixture of high intrinsic load and high extraneous load is the learning equivalent of a fatal cocktail.

Germane load

The third type of cognitive load – germane load – is far more desirable. It is the load placed on working memory that contributes directly to genuine learning. In other words, the nourishing and productive thinking that causes our students to form and consolidate long-term memories. Cognitive load researchers and theorists recommend a healthy diet of reduced extraneous load and increased germane load. Sweller et al. put it like this:

> The combination of decreasing extraneous cognitive load and at the same time increasing germane cognitive load involves redirecting attention: Learners' attention must be withdrawn from processes not relevant to learning and directed toward processes that are relevant to learning and, in particular, toward the construction and mindful abstraction of schemas.[13]

Therefore, in short, we should:

- Remain mindful of intrinsic load.
- Reduce extraneous load.
- Increase germane load.

13 John Sweller et al., Cognitive Architecture and Instructional Design, *Educational Psychology Review* 10(30) (1998): 251–298 at 264. Available at: http://www.csuchico.edu/~nschwartz//Sweller%20van%20 Merrienboer%20and%20Pass%201998.pdf.

Tailoring explanations to cope with the limited capacity of the working memory

How, then, can we use cognitive load theory to improve the way in which we design our explanations of the subject matter? Here are six approaches:

1. Teach bit by bit

The most effective way to reduce intrinsic cognitive load is to break complex material into smaller segments, or parts, and to teach these segments one by one before integrating them into a whole.[14] See the following figure:

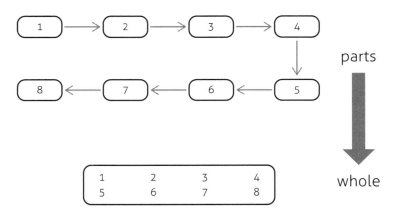

For example, an English class who are learning to write a well-structured story might be taught discrete writing skills first – such as how to write a good opening and ending, how to craft a convincing character or how to create atmosphere through description of a setting – before moving on to write the stories in their entirety. Similarly, a PE teacher might teach each part of the procedure of a tennis serve – from foot position, to racket grip, to follow-through – before allowing students to perform a full serve. According to Barak Rosenshine's study of expert

14 See Edwina Pollock et al., Assimilating Complex Information, *Learning and Instruction* 12(1) (2002): 61–86.

teachers, this approach, which involves presenting information or skills in short bursts and allowing students to practise at each stage, is a key principle of effective teaching practice.[15]

Be that as it may, the bit-by-bit approach can feel counter-intuitive and inauthentic. When we teach new information incrementally, we feel like we are shielding students from a full or true understanding. We find ourselves asking: how can I expect them to understand the true meaning of a concept or idea if I do not allow them to experience it all at once? There is some truth to this concern. If learning is broken into too many segments it can become either too easy or devoid of meaning.

Nonetheless, we must remain mindful of a paradoxical truth: a full and rounded understanding of a multifaceted concept or procedure is rarely reached via a full and rounded teacher explanation of its entirety in one shot. Instead, learning requires a series of base camps and a steady process of acclimatisation. As exhilarating and exciting as a race for the summit is, it is rarely effective – especially for those students with limited prior knowledge of the topic or working memory deficiencies.

2. Funnel attention

The 'split attention effect' is a common source of extraneous cognitive load. Remember, we must reduce extraneous load to allow for effective learning and transfer to long-term memory. According to Chandler and Sweller, it arises when learners are "forced to split their attention between and mentally integrate disparate sources of information".[16] A good example is when diagrams that are required for understanding are presented separately to text – perhaps on different pages of a textbook, on separate worksheets or in different areas of the classroom.

The problem is usually caused when students have to hold one piece of information in working memory while undergoing a visual search for a separate piece of

---

15 Barak Rosenshine, Principles of Instruction: Research-Based Strategies That All Teachers Should Know, *American Educator* 36(1) (2012): 12–19, 39. Available at: https://www.aft.org/sites/default/files/periodicals/Rosenshine.pdf.
16 Paul Chandler and John Sweller, The Split Attention Effect as a Factor in the Design of Instruction, *British Journal of Educational Psychology* 62(2) (1992): 233–246 at 233. Available at: https://onlinelibrary.wiley.com/doi/abs/10.1111/j.2044-8279.1992.tb01017.x.

information. To reduce the split attention effect, we need to reduce unnecessary searching as much as possible and funnel students' attention in one direction. The solutions are usually very simple and can be used to improve slide show design, worksheet design and board work:[17]

- Ensure that labels are integrated into diagrams so that students can look at the text and image simultaneously.

- Limit the number of places in which students need to look for information – when possible, one handout works better than two.

- Use arrows to show connections between text and diagrams.

- Use colour-coding to show the relationships between connected ideas.

- Ensure that information is presented as physically close to related information as possible.[18] This might be on teaching resources, slide shows or a traditional board.

- Use pointing and other hand gestures to direct students' attention towards the salient information.

3. Reduce redundant information

Because working memory capacity is so limited, we should always aim to trim down the amount of information we deliver at once. Put simply, any extra baggage – or extraneous load – should be disposed of. There are two common causes of what is known as the 'redundancy effect': the first is additional information that is not directly relevant to the material being studied; the second comes when the same material is needlessly repeated in multiple forms.

To limit additional information you should:

- Avoid too many asides and digressions when delivering new information – stick to the point.

....

17 See Slava Kalyuga et al., Managing Split-Attention and Redundancy in Multimedia Instruction, *Applied Cognitive Psychology* 13 (1999): 351–371. Available at: https://tecfa.unige.ch/tecfa/teaching/methodo/Kalyuga99.pdf.
18 See Chandler and Sweller, The Split Attention Effect.

- Ensure that inessential images and text are removed from slide shows so that all attention is directed towards the subject matter.

- Refrain from speaking over students while they are thinking and working quietly – they tend to dislike this because they cannot listen to the teacher and process their own thoughts at the same time.

To ensure that information is not needlessly repeated, studies have shown that you should avoid reading aloud text that is written on the board or a slide.[19] This overloads working memory because students cannot process two types of language input simultaneously: in this case, decoding the written text *and* listening to the teacher. One of the forms of input, either the reading or the listening, becomes redundant and actively hampers students' processing of the other.

This advice comes with a number of interesting nuances. The first concerns the complexity of the reading material and the reading proficiency of the students. If the reading material is too difficult for students to access, then it should always be read aloud. Second, spoken delivery appears to be superior to written text for short pieces (no more than two or three sentences); however, this advantage diminishes for longer pieces (full paragraphs and more), where both forms appear to lead to similar learning outcomes.[20] Furthermore, it appears that if students can use text-processing strategies – such as slowing down their reading rate, reading through difficult sections more than once and skipping irrelevant passages – then written text is likely to be more effective than fleeting spoken text.[21] Once again, this relies on adequate levels of reading skill.

Much of the research referenced here was undertaken in unnatural laboratory environments with undergraduate students as participants. However, in one classroom-based study on electronic slide show use, the presentation of on-screen textual information accompanied by spoken narration outperformed text-only and spoken-only presentation.[22] The authors of the study suggest that subtle forms of interference – caused, for example, by taking notes or by the slower processing associated with a more complicated idea – meant that students would struggle to

19 See Kalyuga et al., Managing Split-Attention.
20 Anne Schüler et al., Is Spoken Text Always Better? Investigating the Modality and Redundancy Effect with Longer Text Presentation, *Computers in Human Behaviour* 29(4) (2013): 1590–1601.
21 Schüler et al., Is Spoken Text Always Better?
22 Tzu-Chien Liu et al., Does the Redundancy Effect Exist in Electronic Slideshow Assisted Lecturing?, *Computers and Education* 88 (2015): 303–314.

pay attention to and process the next sentence. By presenting spoken and visual text simultaneously, students had a back-up source to help them to fill in the gaps.

All in all, the evidence on the simultaneous presentation of spoken and visual text is frustratingly ambivalent. However, there is one rock-solid piece of advice that you can take away. *Never expect students to read one thing and listen to another at the same time.* Bizarrely, this still occurs in the classrooms of many experienced teachers. If you are intending to discuss the implications of a written text, then allow ample time for reading first.

4. Limit distraction

Attention is such a precious commodity – which is why distraction is the enemy of the working memory. Your wonderfully lucid explanation of the multiple causes of the English Civil War will be cut to pieces if a boorish Year 9 student decides to break wind midway through your expert unpicking of Charles I's ship money tax. Frustratingly, when an explanation contains multiple related parts, any break in the chain means that you have to start again from scratch. It is impossible for students – especially those with working memory deficiencies – to learn well when the classroom culture means that teacher explanations are regularly interrupted by disruptive behaviour. That's why good behaviour is always a prerequisite for successful explanation.

Putting more obvious behaviour infringements aside, there are a number of subtle forms of distraction to be aware of. Each of these can sever a student's attention:

- A mobile phone vibrating silently in a pocket.
- An adult or student walking in or out of the classroom.
- A sound or commotion from the corridor, another classroom or outside.
- Another student in the class raising their hand midway through an explanation.
- A stimulating display or image on the wall.
- A teacher marching around the room while they are talking.

And the list goes on … In short, it is probably impossible to eliminate all distractions, and it might not always be desirable to do so. However, it is worth remembering this: not only do human beings have a limited working memory capacity but research into the possibility of multitasking shows, categorically, that the human mind cannot think about two things at once, and that attempts to do so lead to poorer performance. And this is true for male *and* female adults and children.[23]

5. Repeat messages and use supports

Teaching is essentially a transient exercise. A piece of information is shared, visually or verbally, before being replaced by another, before being replaced by yet another; the expectation being that students hold all this rapidly accumulating information in their working memory as the teacher ploughs on. We see this phenomenon when a teacher gives a class a long list of instructions to remember or uses a long series of slides that disappear into the ether one by one. These scenarios create the potential for cognitive overload for all students, even those with a larger than average working memory capacity. But they cause particular difficulty for those with reduced working memory capacity. While it is easy to become frustrated as a teacher – it can certainly seem as if some students are wilfully refusing to listen – we must remember that students simply cannot hold, let alone juggle, all that information at once. As teachers, we should always ask two essential questions:

1   How much are my students being expected to hold in their working memory at this point?

2   Is it too much?

There are two strategies that can ease this problem. The first – which all experienced teachers know only too well – is to find every opportunity to repeat task-specific instructions, success criteria and key learning points. You can do this through:

●   Following the time-honoured advice of: first, tell them what you are going to tell them; second, tell them; third, tell them what you have told them.

----

23 See Pedro de Bruyckere et al., *Urban Myths About Learning and Education* [Kindle edn] (London: Academic Press, 2015), loc. 2248–2322.

- Regularly asking students to verbally repeat your instructions – to you or to each other – so that they hear them more than once.

- Reducing the number of instructions and trimming them down to short, single-clause sentences.

The second technique is to use visual, semi-permanent supports and cues to hold the extra information that the working memory is not yet ready for – to outsource it. For instance:

- Instructions and task guidelines that are written up on handouts or permanent displays so that students can refer back to them whenever they need to.

- Slide show notes that are handed out in advance.

- Notes that students have been advised to take at certain points during an earlier part of the lesson.

- Wall displays of key vocabulary, factual knowledge or useful phrases.

However, supports and scaffolds like these should not become a permanent crutch. At some point, they need to be taken away so that students can develop independence and long-term retention.

6. Use worked examples

A worked example is a completed, or partly completed, problem that students can refer to while they are working on a similar one. Worked examples allow students to concentrate on the specific steps they need to follow in order to solve a problem. They are beneficial because they reduce cognitive load and have been shown to be more effective than unguided problem-solving with tasks that involve a number of complex elements (although they are less effective when the problem is less complex or when students have a high level of prior knowledge).[24] They are another example of a semi-permanent memory support. In a sense, a worked example is simply a silent, visual explanation.

---

24 Ouhao Chen et al. The Worked Example Effect, the Generation Effect, and Element Interactivity, *Journal of Educational Psychology* 107(3) (2015): 689–704.

The simplest way to take advantage of the 'worked example effect' is to create a complete answer to a problem and then clearly label the steps that have been taken to solve it. Next to the worked example, provide students with a *similar* problem that has to be solved using the same procedure or method. The worked example provides extra working memory support which avoids cognitive overload. See the following figure:

Worked example	Student practice
Problem/task _____	Problem/task _____

Where possible, try to hide the student practice task while you are talking through the worked example. If you do not, then some students might be tempted to start completing the problem without fully listening to your explanation!

The worked example effect has been shown to be effective in multiple, replicated controlled studies.[25] It can be effective in a range of teaching contexts with a range of different problem types – from measuring the angle of a triangle to writing the introduction to a literary essay. The trick with worked examples is to gradually fade them away so that problems are solved with ever-increasing independence and fewer and fewer teacher-generated cues.

25 John Sweller, The Worked Example Effect and Human Cognition, *Learning and Instruction* 16(2) (2006): 165–169.

Combining words and pictures

An alternative way of limiting cognitive load and enhancing students' learning is offered by what's known as the 'modality effect'. Put simply, this occurs when two modes of communication – auditory and visual – are presented at the same time. At first glance, this suggestion might seem to contradict my earlier assertion that teachers should aim to limit redundant and unnecessary extra input. However, since Baddeley and Hitch's 1974 study, psychologists have theorised that the working memory is divided into two parts – the auditory and the visual. These are known as the 'phonological loop' and the 'visuospatial sketchpad' respectively.[26] The beautiful thing is that they work in tandem without putting extra pressure on overall working memory capacity.

In fact, as Mayer and Moreno assert:

> **meaningful learning occurs when a learner retains relevant information in each store, organizes the information in each store into a coherent representation, and makes connections between corresponding representations in each store ...**[27]

Paivio's dual coding theory offers an even more tantalising prospect: that the combination of verbal and visual messages actually *increases* learning.[28] The effectiveness of a verbal explanation, therefore, will usually be enhanced by the use of relevant visuals – and this is supported by research that covers a wide range of teaching materials, age ranges, contexts and learning outcomes.[29]

So what do we know about the successful application of the modality effect in the classroom?[30]

---

26 Alan D. Baddeley and Graham J. Hitch, Working Memory, in Gordon H. Bower (ed.), *The Psychology of Learning and Motivation*, Vol. 8 (New York: Academic Press, 1974), pp. 47–89.

27 Richard E. Mayer and Roxana Moreno, A Split-Attention Effect in Multimedia Learning: Evidence for Dual Processing Systems in Working Memory, *Journal of Educational Psychology* 90(2) (1998): 312–320 at 312.

28 Allan Paivio, *Imagery and Verbal Processes* (New York: Holt, Rinehart and Winston, 1971).

29 Paul Ginns, Meta-Analysis of the Modality Effect, *Learning and Instruction* 15(4) (2005): 313–331.

30 See Richard E. Mayer, The Five Principles [video]. Available at: https://www.kuleuven.be/english/education/educational-policy/limel/training-platform/script/the-cognitive-theory-of-multimedia-learning.

- Students tend to learn better when images are combined with spoken text rather than when they are combined with written text.

- Even so, visuals do still enhance learning when students are working with longer written texts.

- Spoken text and visuals should always be shared simultaneously rather than one after the other. (This is known as temporal contiguity.)

- It is often helpful to reveal diagrams and images in a gradual, emergent way so that you can direct student attention to the right places and limit cognitive overload. Quite often, this is most effective with a pen and a blank board than with a pre-prepared slide show.

- Use arrows and bold text to funnel students' attention to key words and to the relationships between ideas.

- Avoid irrelevant material – this might include a busy layout, background music or unnecessary facts and figures.

- Related words and images should be presented in close proximity. (This is known as spacial contiguity.)

The modality effect must not be confused with learning styles, the now discredited idea that students learn best when material is presented according to their preferred learning style – visual, auditory or kinaesthetic. Learning styles is one of the most pervasive myths in education and, despite the complete lack of supporting evidence, it remains hard to budge. The truth is that we all learn through visual and auditory means, and combining the two in your explanation is likely to benefit every student in your class. However, some subjects are naturally more visual than others. For example, geography, with its maps and diagrams, is more visual than English or RE. Nevertheless, I think that there is much that teachers of language-based subjects can learn from the modality effect.

RE teacher Jason Ramasami (the illustrator of this book) has developed the extraordinary skill of capturing complex conceptual ideas in a simple and concise visual form. Below are the notes from a lesson on incarnation that Jason created on his tablet in real time and displayed for his class. Note the following design features:

- How simple, clear images are combined with key words and phrases.

- How these are ordered from A to C to direct attention.

- How Jason pre-empts a potential muddling of incarnation and reincarnation.

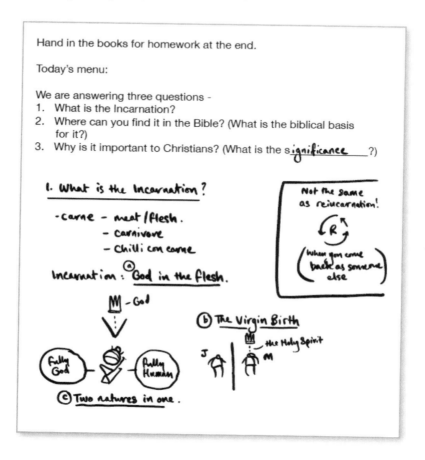

It is important that teachers do not take the guidance from this chapter as an indication that they should copy and paste more clipart to their presentations. Instead, my best advice would be to try to find your own way of representing complex ideas in a visual form, as Jason has done. One approach is to always introduce new vocabulary terms with an accompanying visual image. Another is to represent conceptual ideas through simple geometric diagrams or visual-spatial organisers.

In a lesson covering the theme of individuals versus society in Shakespeare's *Romeo and Juliet*, I used the following two rudimentary images to support my explanation:

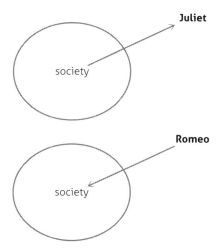

The first image represents how Juliet begins the play as the seemingly archetypal daughter of a high-society family – modest, naïve and conformist. However, as the play progresses, her individual nature asserts itself – causing her to transgress the boundaries imposed upon her by society. The second image represents Romeo's reverse journey from modern man to social conformist. At first, he puts true love before family loyalty; however, as the play progresses, the social expectation that he follow the chivalric code compels him to take revenge for Mercutio's death by killing Tybalt, even though he is likely to lose Juliet as a result. Although in this case both ideas are subject to debate, simple diagrams can provide a concrete way of supporting and suggesting more subtle interpretations.

The perfect slide show

The jury is out as to whether slide shows support or hamper learning. It is likely that when they are used well they enhance it, and when used poorly they add to cognitive overload and diminish it. In some schools, the slide show has become synonymous with the lesson itself. In fact, I have even heard tales of schools in which the senior leadership team expect all lessons to be supported by a slide show. This, of course, is a senseless policy. In most cases, students will learn, or will not learn, irrespective of whether their teacher has used a slide show.

Based on the ideas in this chapter, here are my top ten tips for improving slide shows and board work:

1   Less is more. Reduce the amount of text and diagrams to as little as is necessary.

2   Use slides to *outsource* working memory, not to overload it.

3   Stick to a regular format for every lesson so that students become well-acquainted, and not confused, by your approach.

4   Aim for a simple design.

5   Use images to support complex and conceptual ideas.

6   Ensure that the font size is sufficiently large for all to see easily.

7   Reveal ideas stage by stage on the same slide, rather than on consecutive slides.

8   Talk to the students, not the slide show.

9   Leave room on the slide to add extra workings and annotations.

10 Remember that spoken words and slides are fleeting and transient. Your students' innate cognitive architecture means that they will be unable to hold on to them all at once.

Chapter summary

- When students are new to a topic, explicit instruction is far superior to minimal guidance. However, as they gain in expertise, support should be faded out.

- Students are likely to learn more when the limited capacity of the working memory is catered for. To do this you could: break down complex concepts and procedures into smaller parts; funnel attention towards important material; reduce redundant and superfluous information and images; limit distraction; repeat key messages; and use worked examples for problem-solving tasks.

- The modality effect means that combining auditory and visual input is a particularly powerful teaching method.

First steps

- When planning your next scheme of work, ensure that the first few lessons are teacher-led and then gradually fade out this support as the unit progresses.

- When planning your next lesson, consider the amount of information that students have to hold in their working memory at each stage. Is it too much? Is it too little? How could you adapt the lesson accordingly?

- Take three challenging concepts from your subject. Practise drawing them as diagrams or simple graphics. (Hint: you need not be Leonardo da Vinci or Jason Ramasami to do this effectively!)

Chapter 4
Concepts, examples and misconceptions

Abstract concepts should be supported by concrete examples.

Tyler is an ordinary 15-year-old at an ordinary secondary school. It is Friday. In his maths lesson, he subtracts algebraic fractions. In English, his class discuss tragic structure in Shakespeare's Macbeth. In biology, he looks at communicable and non-communicable diseases, while in geography he covers population density in the UK. And in the final lesson of the day, PE theory, Tyler studies the scientific principles that underpin planning a personal fitness training programme.

Tyler is also very busy at the weekends. On Friday evening, he watches an episode of the cult series *Breaking Bad* (even though he is underage) and pops out to the shop to buy some paracetamol for his younger sister who is curled up on the sofa with a cold. On Saturday, Tyler goes for a run in the countryside on the outskirts of the city where he lives (he is a middle distance runner and is training for a meet next weekend). On Sunday, he finishes his maths homework.

Tyler is an archetypal teenager whose understanding of the world is formed by a combination of school and home life. You have probably already noted the parallels between the academic material he has covered in school and the experiences he has outside it: the TV series *Breaking Bad* echoes the structure of a Shakespearean tragedy through the tragic hero's descent into tyranny; his sister's common cold is an example of a communicable disease; his decision to run in the countryside rather than in the city is influenced by the sheer density of the urban population; and his training programme, designed and insisted upon by his athletics coach, has been informed by the principles of frequency and intensity. His maths learning – on subtracting algebraic equations – has been reinforced through the homework task he has completed.

In short, there is no clear dividing line between the classroom and the world: life is mirrored by education, and education is mirrored by life. However, there are some essential differences between the knowledge gained from personal experience and the abstract knowledge of school. Each student brings very different knowledge into the classroom – some bring more than others and, sometimes, this knowledge is wrong or only partially right.

Linked to this is the reality that the more proficiency a student has in a particular domain (or area of learning), the less mental effort they will need to exert in solving problems in that domain. A fluent reader, for example, can read a Victorian novel or a science textbook without having to decode complex, multisyllable words. A fluent reader can transfer this skill from one subject to another and from one topic to another.

The teacher's central task at all stages of education, then, is to introduce students to knowledge that transcends the individual and the context. We call this conceptual knowledge, and the more academic concepts you can master, the more successfully you will navigate the education system. Concepts also create efficiency; they become intellectual lodestones. By forming the building blocks and reference points of the curriculum, they then support the learning of new and harder concepts.

A concept allows for abstraction. It allows us to generalise from a specific context to many other similar contexts – for example, from population density in the immediate vicinity of Tyler's house to population density in cities across the world. The logical linking together of these abstractions forms the basis of conceptual thought. In many ways, the purpose of school is to help students to see the distance between their personal lives and their academic learning – to understand that their personal, concrete experience is merely a drop in a multitudinous ocean.

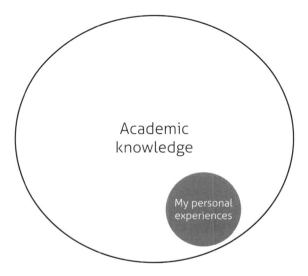

However diverse and vibrant our personal experiences, and however observant and insightful we are, we are unlikely to grasp an academic concept in its fullness and intricacy without some effortful study. And usually this will be introduced by a teacher through a spoken, visual or textual explanation.

Alongside conceptual knowledge, we should also consider the other types of information that students encounter in a school curriculum. Some subjects, such as mathematics and physics, are already abstract and intangible in nature, whereas others, such as geography and biology, are already supported by concrete, everyday examples.

Some of the types of knowledge students have to learn include:

- **Factual knowledge:** true statements about the world – for example, the Battle of Hastings took place in 1066; the radius and ulna are in the forearm; Christians believe that Jesus Christ is the son of God.

- **Scientific knowledge:** a fact that has been acquired through scientific method – for example, the average human body carries ten times more bacterial cells than human cells; the earth is not flat; the earth orbits the sun.

- **Moral knowledge:** our understanding about right and wrong behaviour (relative to the situation and the social group we are part of, and often based on hypothetical thinking) – for example, it is wrong to hurt others; it is right to help those who are less fortunate than ourselves; it is right to treat others as we would like to be treated ourselves.

- **Aesthetic knowledge:** our private understanding of what makes something beautiful or not – for example, to be moved or horrified by Picasso's Guernica; to appreciate the perfection of a Shakespearean sonnet; to find insights in the way the world is understood differently in the French language.

- **Procedural (practical) knowledge:** knowledge required to perform a skill – for example, to know how to bowl a cricket ball; how to set out a formal letter; how to solve a geometry problem.

- **Metacognitive knowledge:** knowledge required to think about one's own learning more explicitly – for example, strategies for planning, monitoring and evaluating extended writing; strategies for revising in the lead-up to an exam.

These types of knowledge have differing levels of significance depending on the subject. If the purpose of a subject is to provide a window to some kind of scientific, moral or aesthetic 'truth', then the search for this truth takes many different paths. All subjects are supported by factual knowledge and require the development of procedural knowledge, whereas subjects like English literature and art hinge upon aesthetic judgement, and RE is formed from moral and ethical principles. Needless to say, it takes an incredibly skilled teacher to help a child to transform their perception of beauty or influence their moral judgement of a situation.

Put simply, the inherent nature of conceptual understanding is different between and within every subject. For instance, a successful piece of narrative writing in English requires a well-developed appreciation of different types of knowledge, and the ability to explore the following questions:

- Is the setting and context of my writing true to the *factual* and *scientific* world?

- To what extent do my characters comply with or break the *moral* conventions of society?

- Is the style and structure of my story *aesthetically pleasing*?

- Do I know *how* to structure a story in a successful way?

- How will I *plan* my writing before I start and *evaluate* it after I have finished?

In the rest of this chapter, we will explore practical ways to help students untangle their personal experiences from the factual, scientific, moral, aesthetic, procedural and metacognitive concepts that they must master in our classrooms. The Russian psychologist Lev Vygotsky once wrote: "with the help of the concept, we are able to penetrate through the external appearance of phenomena to penetrate into their essence".[1] If we explain these concepts well, then we will not only transform the way in which students view the everyday world, but also their chances of academic success.

Why are examples so important?

If conceptual knowledge is so pivotal to learning, then why should we concern ourselves with examples? Why should we waste our time on factual information when an understanding of the general principle is the greater goal? Cognitive scientist Daniel Willingham distils many years of research findings into one sentence: "We understand new things in the context of things we already know, and

---

1   Quoted in Jan Derry, *Vygotsky: Philosophy and Education* (Chichester: Wiley-Blackwell, 2013). p. 21.

most of what we know is concrete."[2] He goes on to write that the best way "to help students understand an abstraction is to expose them to many different versions of the abstraction".[3] In other words, surface-level examples are crucial to the development of deep-level processing and understanding.

It is almost impossible to 'get' a new concept without first being exposed to an example of that concept at work in the real world. This is why the concept of revolution in history is best taught through historical events and contexts: the French Revolution, the Russian Revolution or even the Industrial Revolution. In the early stages of learning, the more concrete the example, the better. This does not mean that we should avoid abstractions altogether. Instead it means that we should explain mysterious objects, forces and phenomena in a way that would make them tangible. To do this, we must pepper our explanations with real-world referents.

There are two possible ways of guaranteeing that this happens. The first might be to ensure that students learn through direct, first-hand experiences – for example, through field trips and museum visits. As enjoyable as these experiences can be, sadly this direct approach would be an incredibly expensive and impractical way of running an education system. Trips are only ever an added bonus. So the second approach is to ensure that students experience the real world through indirect experiences. Virtual experiences of learning – through personal reading or a teacher-initiated episode – can be as powerful as direct experiences. A trip to the forest will allow for many beautiful and powerful sensory experiences: the dank aroma of leaf mould, the spongy brilliant-green of moss, the trilling tune of a wood warbler ... But, ultimately, learning is a result of the thinking that occurs in the working memory. With good teaching, children can learn about the ecosystem of a forest in the classroom too.[4]

---

2 Willingham, *Why Don't Students Like School?*, p. 67.
3 Willingham, *Why Don't Students Like School?*, p. 67.
4 See Robert J. Marzano, *Building Background Knowledge for Academic Achievement: Research on What Works in Schools* (Alexandria, VA: Association for Supervision and Curriculum Development, 2004) for an interesting discussion on the impact of direct experiences and indirect experiences.

The perfect example

Designing good examples is an art form in its own right. The perfect example is simple and self-contained; it provides an effortless shortcut to understanding. Effective examples not only bring insight and clarity, but also accentuate the inherent personality of the material too. They can inject a topic with emotion, humour, absurdity, poignancy or a sense of the unexpected. They breathe new life into potentially stagnant ideas. It takes many years for an expert teacher to nurture and prune their collection of examples, but once they have, teaching becomes a craft performed with wonderful deftness and ease.

So, what makes for a good example?

- It should connect to what a student *already knows*.

- It should be as *simple* as possible.

- It should appeal to the *senses*.

- It should be easy to *transfer* to new contexts.

- It should be *memorable*.

- It should come in *multiples*.

- It should aim to provoke an *emotional* response.

The writer Bill Bryson puts each of these principles to work with aplomb in *A Short History of Nearly Everything*, a science book for beginners. To explain the conservation of mass, for example, Bryson gives the example: "If you burned this book now, its matter would be changed to ash and smoke, but the net amount of stuff in the universe would be the same."[5] This little sentence provided something of a Eureka moment for me. It used something tangible – the book I was holding. It was simple. It was tactile. And it helped me to transfer the concept of conservation of mass to other objects: my own body after death, for example. Matter is indestructible, and so the atoms that make up my body will simply take on new arrangements in new places; they will not be lost forever.

---

5   Bill Bryson, *A Short History of Nearly Everything: A Journey through Space and Time* (London: Black Swan, 2016), p. 134.

Later in the book, Bryson helps his reader to imagine the unimaginable: the fact that at sea level and at 0° Celsius, one cubic centimetre of air (the size of a sugar cube) contains forty-five billion billion molecules:

> **Think how many cubic centimetres there are in the world outside your window – how many sugar cubes it would take to fill that view. Then think how many it would take to build a universe. Atoms, in short, are very abundant.[6]**

Again, Bryson's example is perfect in its simplicity: everyone can picture the size of a sugar cube; it hinges on a visual representation and is an instantly memorable image.

However, these examples do not capture the entirety of the concepts that are being explained. This is worth noting and is especially relevant to teachers whose students work with very complex concepts. A single example only provides a simplified and partial representation of the whole. An isolated example can lead to a situation where students struggle to fully separate the concept from the presentation. This causes the surface features of the representation to become muddled with the deep structure of the concept, or problem, at hand. For example, the Bill Bryson examples could lead some readers to develop misconceptions: that molecules are only present in the air or that conservation of matter only occurs when an object is burnt, for example. In these cases, the example has provided a useful bridge between current knowledge of the world and the strange new world of the unfamiliar academic idea, but it has also caused mislearning of the essential principle.

A way to counterbalance this problem is to always come armed with multiple examples. In fact, evidence from the science of learning suggests that students are more likely to be able to transfer learning to new contexts when they are given two examples rather than one.[7] Once a student has grasped the basics of a new idea, they have to discern the defining aspects of the concept so that they can build the depth and accuracy of their understanding. The broader the range of contrasting and interesting examples, the easier they will find it to make accurate generalisations and extrapolations.

----

6   Bryson, *A Short History of Nearly Everything*, p. 176.
7   See this guest blog post for more: Althea Bauernschmidt, Two Examples Are Better Than One, *The Learning Scientists* [blog] (30 May 2017). Available at: http://www.learningscientists.org/blog/2017/5/30-1.

There are many useful methods for improving the way in which you present multiple examples. One is to present the same concept across a *range of very different contexts*. This helps students to understand when and where the concept can be generalised. Another is to present *small and subtle variations* on the same concept to tease out exceptions and subtle nuances. For example, an English teacher might present these two sets of examples when introducing the possessive apostrophe:

Set 1 – range of contexts

- Kathryn's gloves were soaked.

- My dog's bark is very deep.

- The cat's eyes gleamed wickedly.

- The tree's height was extraordinary.

- My mum is my great-grandfather's son's daughter.

Set 2 – small variations

- They were Andrew's gloves.

- The gloves were Andrew's.

- We visited Andrew's house.

- I'm going to Andrew's tonight.

- There were two Andrews living there.

Set 1 shows us that apostrophe of possession rules hold fast in a range of scenarios. Set 2 presents a number of subtle variations on the same theme and allows the teacher to pre-empt areas of potential confusion and exceptions to the rule. For example, in the fourth sentence, although the word 'house' is missing, it is implied – and so the apostrophe of possession rule should still be applied.

Perhaps a golden rule for teachers is to always have as many examples as possible at the ready. With simple concepts, the whole class or individual students will need only one or two; with tricky concepts, they may need many more.

Examples and non-examples

If there is one strategy in this chapter that will help all students to learn better, it is this: introduce new concepts through contrasting examples *and* non-examples. According to Wragg and Brown, 'not-examples' (or non-examples) are "cases which do not meet the criteria of the concept, but then, by comparison, illustrate what the real criteria for inclusion in the concept actually are".[8] Non-examples are particularly useful because they prevent students overgeneralising and encourage them to discriminate between similar concepts. All teachers and parents will be familiar with the tendency among novice learners to overgeneralise. We see this when a young child misuses the past tense '-ed' rule with an irregular verb: "I *knowed* you would do that!" Or perhaps in maths when a child believes that if 5 x 11 = 55 and 9 x 11 = 99, then 11 x 11 must be 111. We can all become better teachers if we learn how to avert misconceptions before they take root.

In my English lessons, I tend to introduce grammatical concepts, such as the correct use of the semicolon, through examples and non-examples. For example:

1   Tom was unhappy; Arsenal had lost that day. (tick)

2   The tiger is a ferocious predator; it can kill an animal twice its size. (tick)

3   The winter is the most depressing time of year; the summer is full of joy. (tick)

---

8   Edward C. Wragg and George Brown, *Explaining* (London and New York: Routledge, 1993), p. 33.

4   Julian is my closest friend; and I can never be apart from him. (cross)

5   Even though I am a Tottenham fan; I have a soft spot for Brighton & Hove Albion. (cross)

The non-examples are based upon the common mistakes and misconceptions that I see regularly in student writing. In example 4 the conjunction 'and' is redundant and in example 5 the semicolon has been used erroneously to separate a subordinate clause from a main clause.

Teachers often worry that by presenting accurate examples and misconceptions together the boundaries between right and wrong will become blurred and, in turn, that this will lead to students learning the misconception and not the rule – the so-called 'backfire effect'. We are right to be concerned about this – but there are some simple ways around the problem:

● Start by making it very clear why 'right is right'.

● Direct students towards the misconception and explain clearly why it is wrong – "This is incorrect because …"

● Circle back to the misconception as often as you can and ask students to explain to you why it is wrong.

● Design tasks that allow the class to discriminate between examples and non-examples – for example, using classification tasks or Venn diagrams.

● Design a memorable cue that reminds students of the common mistake.

● Encourage students to create their own examples and non-examples.

Must haves and may haves

Concepts are also defined according to 'must have' and 'may have' attributes. Must have attributes are those features that are critical to a concept; it cannot exist without them. For instance, a Shakespearean tragedy must end with a catastrophe; a pentagon must have five sides; a volcano must have an opening in the surface of the earth. On the other hand, may have attributes apply in some cases of the concept, but not all. Some Shakespearean tragedies are about thwarted love; some pentagons contain sides of irregular length; some volcanoes are conical in shape.

Wragg and Brown provide an incredibly useful framework for explaining concepts.[9] I call it the 'concept template' and it includes the following elements:

1 A label or name – the word (or words) used to name the concept.

2 A simple definition.

3 A list of attributes.

   i   must have

   ii may have

4 A list of examples.

   i   illustrative examples

   ii non-examples

. . . .

9 Wragg and Brown, *Explaining*, p. 33.

The concept of 'mammals' might look like this:

Name	mammals
Definition	Mammals are animals such as humans, dogs, lions and whales. In general, female mammals give birth to babies rather than laying eggs, and feed their young with milk.[10]
Attributes	
must have	Hair or fur at some stage of the life cycle; mammary glands in females; single-boned lower jaws; warm-blooded metabolisms; diaphragms; four-chambered hearts; three-bones in the middle ear.
may have	Breast-feeding males (Dayak fruit bat); the ability to fly (bat); an aquatic habitat (whale); a land habitat; seven neck vertebrae; four legs.
Examples	
illustrative examples	Human beings; elephants; whales; bats; dolphins; hedgehogs; seals; platypuses; kangaroos.
non-examples	All birds; all fish; scorpions (arachnids); lizards (reptiles); frogs (amphibians); woodlice (isopod land crustaceans).

A template like this can be used to plan teacher explanations and questions. You might ask students to fill in a blank version before you teach a topic, to assess their prior knowledge and identify any misconceptions. Similarly, students can complete them once their knowledge and understanding becomes more proficient.

In less scientific subjects, such as English literature and history, the boundaries between concepts and ideas are sometimes very indistinct or open to interpretation. In these subjects, you might experiment with the layout and the wording of the template. For example, in my English literature lessons I put a different spin on

---

10 See https://www.collinsdictionary.com/dictionary/english/mammal.

this structure to help my students to investigate complex characterisation. To do this, we use these headings to explore each main character in a text: name, factual examples, always shows, sometimes shows, never shows.

A concept is similar to an iceberg. Often our students can only see the part that rises above the waterline; they do not realise that a deeper, fuller and usually more subtle truth lies beneath. Great explanation rests on a teacher's ability and willingness to guide students towards the murky, uncomfortable and sometimes contradictory nature of truth. Many concepts in education are hard to teach and hard to learn. Too often, teachers move too quickly through lessons and the curriculum without leaving time for real investigation. All teachers should heed the words of Friar Lawrence from Shakespeare's *Romeo and Juliet*: "Wisely and slow; they stumble that run fast."

The strategy of helping students to see the distinction between essential and non-essential elements is also driven by a moral imperative. It helps to challenge deep-rooted bias and promotes the kind of finely tuned discrimination that distinguishes balanced intellectual thinking from oversimplified thinking. Quite simply, not all snakes are venomous, not all teenagers are insolent and not all homeless people are drug addicts. Indeed the type of careful thinking we need from our students has taken on extra importance in recent years. In a world of deplorable fake news, ubiquitous smartphones and persistent xenophobia, it is essential that schools teach young people the disciplined habits of mind that will protect them from jumping to easy, simplistic and erroneous binary conclusions in their adulthood.

When exemplification goes wrong

Ultimately, the role of an example is to provide a stepping stone towards understanding and knowledge. Unfortunately, as with all aspects of teaching, an example can sometimes have a different effect to the one the teacher intended. An awkward example can cause shallow understanding and, in the worst cases, create confusion or lead to misconceptions. The table below explores some common errors and outlines ways to rectify them:

Error	Problem	Solution
Too few examples.	This can lead to a shallow understanding of the boundaries of the concept.	Start with simple, everyday examples to connect with prior knowledge. Then start to introduce less obvious cases, exceptions and caveats, before moving on to non-examples that appear to blur into related concepts at first glance.
Too little scrutiny of examples.	Sometimes teachers assume that students have fully understood a concept when they have not.	Your aim is to gain as much real-time feedback as you can of how the class (and individual students) are modelling the concept for themselves. Frequent questioning allows you to track their understanding and nip potential misconceptions in the bud. Stock questions and prompts might include: "Why is this right?" "Why is this wrong?" "How does x connect with y?" "Tell me what you don't understand."

Error	Problem	Solution
Examples are too complicated or abstract.	If examples refer to situations and scenarios way beyond a student's prior knowledge and experience, then it is very unlikely that they will be in a position to construct an accurate and true understanding of the concept.	Make sure your examples contain simple real-world referents. Ensure that these are likely to be within your students' frame of reference. While common cultural reference points – films, television, sport, etc. – are useful, remember that the interests and personal experiences of your students will be varied.
Concepts are too indistinct.	Students (and adults) get muddled between similar concepts – for example, area and perimeter in mathematics; simile and metaphor in English; stalactites and stalagmites in science.	In this common situation, the problem is caused by fuzzy boundaries between concepts rather than by the examples themselves. The trick here is to provide very distinct memory cues at the point of teaching. A recommended approach would be to: ● Make the class aware from the start that the two concepts are often confused. ● Teach a visual mnemonic to remember the difference – for example, stalactites hang from the ceiling of a cave like tights hanging on a washing line. ● Ensure that students practise using the mnemonic so that it is not forgotten.

How concrete examples can improve memory retention

Fifty years of research shows us that human beings are more likely to remember concrete examples than abstract ones. For example, Gorman found that concrete nouns like 'button' were easier to remember than words like 'bound'.[11]

Weinstein et al. advise that as well as helping with retention, paired concrete examples help students to transfer their understanding to new contexts (the holy grail of learning):

> providing concrete examples during instruction should improve retention of related abstract concepts, rather than the concrete examples alone being remembered better ... Having students actively explain how two examples are similar and encouraging them to extract the underlying structure on their own can also help with transfer.[12]

A valid concern regarding the use of concrete examples is that playful, humorous or fun examples could prove to be counterproductive. In other words, the students remember your wonderfully delivered witty joke instead of the concept you were elucidating! The good news is that fun, or even risqué, examples do not appear to harm learning. In fact, as long as they are relevant to the concept and do not include too much extraneous detail, the evidence suggests that they provide an extra memory boost.[13] This is excellent news for teachers: it is a much-needed licence for creativity.

If you need help to find amusing and memorable examples, the Internet offers a smorgasbord of delights. In recent years, my teaching of grammatical concepts has

---

11 A. M. Gorman, Recognition Memory for Nouns as a Function of Abstractedness and Frequency, *Journal of Experimental Psychology* 61 (1961): 23–39.

12 Yana Weinstein et al., Teaching the Science of Learning, *Cognitive Research: Principles and Implications* 3(2) (2018): 1–17 at 11. Available at: https://cognitiveresearchjournal.springeropen.com/articles/10.1186/s41235-017-0087-y.

13 Weinstein et al., Teaching the Science of Learning.

become more vibrant and interesting with the use of examples that I have found online. To help students avoid dangling modifiers, I use these:

Early men hunted mammoths with spears.

I found my missing hat cleaning my room.

To help students to understand when an Oxford comma would be appropriate, we compare the following:

We invited the dogs, William, and Harry. (With the Oxford comma.)

We invited the dogs, William and Harry. (Without it.)

It is also important that we invest time in helping our students to memorise concrete examples. This process is often overlooked. The definition of a dangling modifier is "a grammatical error where the modifying word or phrase is attached to the wrong subject or where the subject is missing in a sentence".[14] This abstract definition is hard to conceptualise and even harder to apply to your own writing. Memorising it is a waste of time. It is far better to ensure that a student memorises a few examples (including the mammoth and hat ones) so that the next time they edit their own writing and notice a similar error they think: "Ah, that's like the mammoth example Sir showed us; I need to change this sentence." Ultimately, a concrete example provides us with a memorable support structure that helps us to reconstruct an abstract construct in our minds when we need to.

A useful tip is to conduct a pre-mortem for each lesson: if my students do not remember this in six months' time, what will have caused this? Planning distinct and lively examples is one of the first steps towards long-term retention.

---

14 See https://www.grammarly.com/blog/how-to-eliminate-dangling-modifiers-from-your-writing/.

Tackling misconceptions

We have already touched on the notion of misconceptions on a number of occasions in this chapter. Students come to lessons with pre-existing schemas (organised frameworks of knowledge) that represent the world as they see it; some of these are accurate conceptions, others are illogical or erroneous. Even though these alternative conceptions are frustrating for teachers, they are a natural part of life and learning and they often derive from common sense or intuitive thinking about the natural world. Misconceptions are prevalent in every subject, but they are especially rife in the sciences. Students often arrive in physics lessons believing that energy is created and then destroyed rather than being transferred from one form to another, or in chemistry lessons convinced that there is air between the particles in a gas. Thankfully, there are many common, shared misconceptions, like these two examples, that experienced teachers can learn to pre-empt.

On other occasions, individual students develop rather unusual or idiosyncratic misconceptions. I once taught a very high-achieving Year 11 student (who has since won a scholarship to a prestigious independent school) who was completely convinced that the word perhaps was spelt *prehaps* – even in the face of irrefutable dictionary evidence!

This introduces another common problem that teachers have to solve: that misconceptions are extremely tenacious and have extraordinary staying power. Chinn and Brewer describe seven different responses that people – children *and* adults – have when encountering anomalous data (that which cannot be explained by our pre-existing understanding of the world).[15]

These are:

1   *Ignore it* completely.

2   *Reject it* by arguing that the data is wrong or simply fraudulent.

3   *Exclude it* by conveniently segregating the theories learnt in school from everyday theories of how the real world works.

....

15 Clark A. Chinn and William F. Brewer, The Role of Anomalous Data in Knowledge Acquisition: A Theoretical Framework and Implications for Science Instruction, *Review of Educational Research* 63(1) (1993): 1–49. Available at: http://journals.sagepub.com/doi/10.3102/00346543063001001.

4 *Hold it* in abeyance by putting the problem to one side and assuming that someone will prove us right at some point in the future.

5 *Reinterpret it* by accepting the new data but explaining it according to our existing theory.

6 Make a *peripheral change* to our existing theory without destroying its core beliefs.

7 Change to a *new theory* and reject our existing hypothesis.

As you will have noticed, only the seventh option – theory change – produces a desirable outcome. Misconceptions are limpet-like. They are embedded onto the very fabric of our students' beliefs about the physical and cultural world they inhabit and, as such, they are devilishly difficult to budge. Even if a child's verbal answers and written work demonstrate surface-level understanding of the concept they have been taught, this does not necessarily indicate an ontological change in the way they now think about the world. Despite successfully answering the questions in a plenary quiz at the end of a lesson, they may skip down the corridor still holding the belief that the seasons are caused by the earth's distance from the sun rather than by the earth's axial tilt! The child's central beliefs, therefore, remain untouched by scientific proof.

How, then, can teachers get better at helping students to shed their misconceptions? First, many studies suggest that standard forms of teaching, such as lectures, discovery-based learning and simply reading a text, cannot be solely relied upon to effect conceptual change. More subtle methods, including the following, are more likely to be fruitful:[16]

● Before teaching a new topic, give students a task which helps to identify their pre-existing misconceptions. Once they have taken on board new concepts, they can then refer back to it to see how far they have come.

● Ensure that new theories are always presented with plausible and clear examples.

● Use model-based reasoning or thought experiments to help students to construct representations of the world outside their everyday experience.

16 See Joan Lucariello and David Naff, How Do I Get My Students Over Their Alternative Conceptions (Misconceptions) for Learning?, *American Psychological Association* [blog]. Available at: http://www.apa.org/education/k12/misconceptions.aspx for more detail.

For instance, Isaac Newton visualised a cannon being fired on top of a high mountain to show that gravity is universal and that it is a key force in planetary motion. Without the force of gravitation, the cannonball would shoot off in a straight line away from earth. Such hypothetical thought experiments give plausibility to potentially abstract concepts.

● Create cognitive conflict by presenting students with situations and scenarios that are incongruous with their current conceptions. You can do this by presenting a refutational text which introduces the misconception, refutes it and then provides the new and satisfactory theory. This should then lead to discussions and activities that allow the students to see the conflict between the two. However, some studies suggest that this method is more effective with higher-attaining than lower-attaining students, for whom a more traditional direct teaching approach is more successful.[17]

● As suggested throughout this chapter, use real-world case studies to bring concepts to life.[18]

All in all, the entrenched nature of misconceptions is one of teaching's greatest challenges. Teacher training and CPD is most effective when it retains a strong focus on the correction of common mistakes and misconceptions. Subject departments should make it their mission to identify the most problematic misconceptions in the discipline, record them centrally and share the most effective strategies for helping students to overcome them.

Chapter summary

● The end goal of teaching is the development of students' conceptual knowledge; however, this is best achieved though concrete, memorable real-world examples.

● Effective explanation of concepts involves the presentation of examples, non-examples and must and may have attributes.

---

17 Anat Zohar and Simcha Aharon-Kravetsky, Exploring the Effects of Cognitive Conflict and Direct Teaching for Students of Different Academic Levels, *Journal of Research in Science Teaching* 42(7) (2005): 829–855.
18 Yildizay Ayyildiz and Leman Tarhan, Case Study Applications in Chemistry Lesson: Gases, Liquids, and Solids, *Chemistry Education Research and Practice* 14(4) (2013): 408–420.

- Students' misconceptions are tenacious and stubborn. Teachers, departments and schools should maintain a relentless focus on helping students to overcome them.

First steps

- Design a concept template for a topic you are due to teach next half term. Alongside it, create a list of verbal questions you will use to assess and probe students' understanding of this concept.

- Make a list of the ten most common errors, misunderstandings and misconceptions you have noticed in your students' thinking.

- Start creating a list of useful and effective examples to overcome these. Ask experienced colleagues to contribute to this list.

Chapter 5

Metaphor and analogy

Connections should be forged between students' prior knowledge and the material to be learnt.

As we have already established, the technical and conceptual language of the classroom is difficult to grasp. What to the expert teacher feels like a precise and accurate explanation of a new concept can to the novice student feel like a lifeless and alien mishmash of words and ideas. This is most especially true for those students who have had little exposure to academic language in their family lives outside school, for whom even learning in their own language too often feels like operating in an unfamiliar foreign tongue.

This problem can be illustrated by looking at dictionary definitions of scientific concepts:

Osmosis: a process by which molecules of a solvent tend to pass through a semipermeable membrane from a less concentrated solution into a more concentrated one.[1]

Autotroph: an organism that is able to form nutritional organic substances from simple inorganic substances such as carbon dioxide.[2]

For those of us unfamiliar with the dense vocabulary of the scientific world, these definitions are tricky to conceptualise. Imagine how hard it is for students when definitions – in any subject – are presented in this pared-down fashion. To begin to understand 'osmosis' and 'autotroph' we need to have prior knowledge of the meanings of the words 'molecule', 'solvent' and 'inorganic'. We also need to create a mental model – a sort of distilled interweaving of words and images – that allows us to make sense of the interaction between these concepts. It is no wonder, then, that introducing new vocabulary through dictionary definitions has been shown to be a very ineffective way of teaching new terminology.[3] There is an uncomfortable paradox at work here. The kinds of explanations that contain the entirety of a new idea with accuracy and precision are not the kinds of explanations that usually help children to successfully imagine new and complex ideas. Connections should be forged *between* students' prior knowledge and the material to be learnt, and, to this end, many young people require a bridge – one that spans from the palpable and familiar world of the known to the mysterious realm of the unknown. We call this metaphor.

1   See https://en.oxforddictionaries.com/definition/osmosis.
2   See https://en.oxforddictionaries.com/definition/autotroph.
3   Isabel L. Beck et al., *Bringing Words to Life: Robust Vocabulary Instruction* (New York: Guilford Press, 2002).

A metaphor is when one thing is used to stand for, or symbolise, something else – for example, "Juliet is the sun", "silence is golden" or "life is like a box of chocolates". As George Lakoff and Mark Johnson, authors of the influential *Metaphors We Live By*, put it: "The essence of metaphor is understanding and experiencing one kind of thing in terms of another."[4] A metaphor must contain a *target* and a *source*. The target is the concept that we are aiming to understand better: Juliet, silence or life. The source is taken from a different domain and helps us to improve our understanding of the target: in this case, the sun, golden and a box of chocolates. Usually the target is an abstract idea whereas the source is a more concrete real-world referent. We make sense of a metaphor by mapping out the things that the target and the source have in common. A box of chocolates, for instance, offers up variety, sweetness, surprise and sometimes bitter disappointment – just like the experience of living a complete human life. A pertinent metaphor provides a distinctive and memorable insight into the target, triggering a blossoming of meaning and understanding.

There are various forms of metaphor. A *simile* is when the target and source take the form of a comparison: "as blind as a bat" and "I slept like a log". *Personification* means giving human characteristics to a non-human object or animal: "traffic

---

4   George Lakoff and Mark Johnson, *Metaphors We Live By* (London and Chicago: University of Chicago Press, 1980), p. 5.

slowed to a crawl" and "the wind howled". The *analogy*, however, is a slightly different kettle of fish (note the metaphoric figure of speech!). An analogy forms a logical argument to show the correspondences between a complex idea and a more readily understood one. To illustrate the evolution of modern English, a teacher might use the analogy of a river: single tributaries – Celtic, Latin, Anglo-Saxon, Norse, Norman, French and languages from the Empire, such as Hindi – all flow into one tumultuous torrent, otherwise known as modern British English.

Science writing brims with metaphor and analogy. Think black hole, dwarf planet, the Big Bang and the selfish gene. However, a fierce debate rages about the utility and appropriateness of the use of such metaphors. Some scientists contend that we should 'stick to the numbers' and that clumsy metaphors misrepresent and simplify the facts, giving rise to avoidable misconceptions. Others, such as Timothy Leary, the author of the deliciously metaphoric *Gravity's Engines*, have no problem:

> with the notion of making mental labels for natural phenomena that include some degree of personality. I like my black holes fearsome and my interstellar gas thin and frail. It may well be that in doing so one reinforces a certain blinkering, but we're not all Mr Spock.[5]

Even though metaphors only provide part of the truth, they give us something to grab hold of and relate to physical and emotional experience. The metaphors we use, therefore, are vital in helping our students to connect new concepts to their often limited prior knowledge – like a sort of mental Velcro. They also work like olive branches. A pertinent metaphor takes a student by the hand and invites them to make peace with new understanding, even if the new idea contradicts or blurs their earlier understanding of the world.

---

5   Timothy Leary, In Defense of Metaphors in Science Writing, *Scientific American* [blog] (9 July 2013). Available at: https://blogs.scientificamerican.com/life-unbounded/in-defense-of-metaphors-in-science-writing/.

Into the classroom

Ultimately, a good metaphor operates in the fertile breeding ground between the familiar and the unfamiliar, helping a person to form a relationship with a new idea or concept.

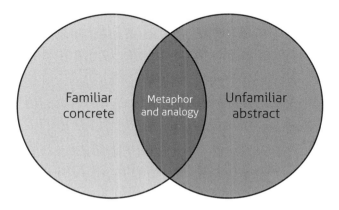

It is important to remember that a metaphor or analogy provides a model of the truth but not the truth itself. To some extent a metaphor is always inaccurate; however, the most apt teaching metaphors are *usefully wrong*. The insight and perception they generate outweighs their potential to create misconceptions. As such, they are most effective when used at the introductory phase of learning – or as distinct labels to improve the retrieval of new memories.

Effective metaphors have four attributes: they are transformative, relevant, distinct and visual.

Transformative metaphors

The best metaphors transform the way in which we perceive the world. They give us new eyes with which to see a subject afresh. Last year I read Jonathan Haidt's wonderful book *The Happiness Hypothesis*, which shares the finding from moral psychology that human decision-making is controlled by two competing forces: the elephant and the rider.[6] The rider represents our analytical, controlled and rational side, whereas the elephant is our emotional, automatic and irrational alter ego. The elephant is a well-chosen metaphor: it is impulsive, instinctive and has the capacity to throw off the much weaker rider with ease. Haidt's argument is that we human beings are far less rational than we tend to believe, and that all of us have an irrational inner elephant that can wreak havoc over the best-laid plans of our inner rider. Now, every time I am tempted to buy a chocolate bar in the newsagent, I see the image of my hapless rider attempting to control the urges of my dominant elephant. In other words, Haidt's mental model has transformed the way in which I see the world – although, unfortunately, my health-conscious rider does not always dissuade my cocoa-loving elephant from guzzling yet another chocolate bar!

In the classroom, a transformative metaphor leads a student across a threshold of understanding and helps them to imagine a concept they would not have encountered through ordinary experience. A transformative metaphor should also be enduring enough to remember and easy to apply to novel scenarios. For example, a primary teacher might start her human biology lesson with the idea that cells are like tiny Lego blocks that are connected to make living things. It is a startlingly simple idea – so simple that the next time a child looks into their garden they might imagine the plants, trees, birds and squirrels as moving, multicoloured assemblages of Lego blocks. Their way of seeing the world, therefore, has been meaningfully altered.

---

6   Jonathan Haidt, *The Happiness Hypothesis: Putting Ancient Wisdom to the Test of Modern Science* (London: Arrow Books, 2006).

In English literature and drama, the 'fourth wall' is the imaginary barrier between the characters in a play and the audience (so called in addition to the three physical walls of the stage). A character who breaks the fourth wall is one who recognises their fictional nature and reaches out to communicate directly with the audience. A student who understands this idea will recognise it the next time they are playing a video game and a character speaks to them through the fourth wall of the screen.

Some transformative metaphors support procedural knowledge as well as conceptual knowledge. These make it easier to think metacognitively about complicated processes and procedures, such as the structure of extended writing. One of my favourites is 'zoom in then zoom out', a phrase I have borrowed from David Didau to teach students how to structure the interplay between analytical and evaluative ideas in an English literature essay. They should 'zoom in' to pinpoint examples from the text, and 'zoom out' to make connections with the text's social and historical context.[7] The simple comparison with filmmaking is easy to remember and apply in the white heat of the exam hall.

7   David Didau, Zooming In and Out, *The Learning Spy* [blog] (11 July 2011). Available at: http://www. learningspy.co.uk/english-gcse/zooming-in-and-out/.

Relevant metaphors

In our 2015 book *Making Every Lesson Count*, Shaun Allison and I gave an example of an analogy that could be used in a physics lesson:

> to demonstrate that a hydrogen atom contains one proton in the nucleus and is surrounded by one electron, science teachers will ask students to imagine a grain of rice in a sports stadium. If the grain – the proton – is placed in the middle of the pitch, the outer row of seats are the limit of the electron's influence, while the remainder of the atom is empty space. Like the rest of the seats, the electron seems to be everywhere at once.[8]

At the time, we were pleased with this analogy: it seemed precise and easy to conceptualise. However, since writing the book, we have been approached by a few science teachers who told us that they had tried out the analogy and it did not work with their class. Why? First, because many of their students had never visited a sports stadium and so had no way of conceptualising the size and shape. Second, sports stadiums come in so many different guises anyway that the source is too vague to be useful – think of a cycling velodrome in comparison with Wembley Stadium. The best metaphors, therefore, must work for everyone in the class, from the most privileged to the most socially disadvantaged.

One teacher we know has designed a far better alternative to our original suggestion: the grain becomes a mote of dust, and the sports stadium becomes the school tennis court. In his classroom, his students can pick out motes of dust in the sunlight and can see the school tennis court from where they sit. There is much less confusion and misunderstanding when he explains it this way. This situation offers a useful lesson: the success of a metaphor or analogy is highly contingent on understanding the environmental context that it is applied to.

The source of your metaphor or analogy should always be a shared point of reference. The concentric diagram that fellows is useful in helping you to choose and invent relevant sources for your analogies and metaphors. The closer you are to the centre, the more likely it is your metaphor will hit the mark.

8   Shaun Allison and Andy Tharby, *Making Every Lesson Count: Six Principles to Support Great Teaching and Learning* (Carmarthen: Crown House Publishing, 2015), p. 73.

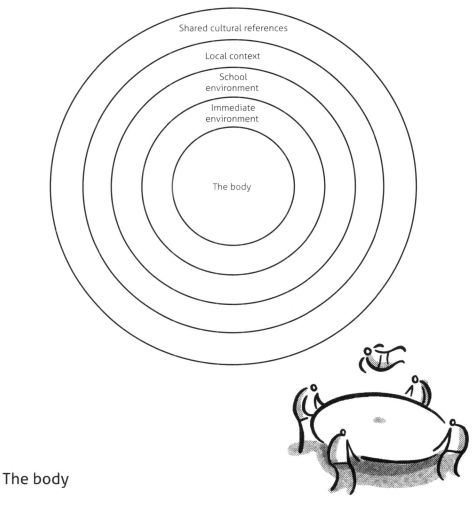

The body

Embodied cognition is the idea that our bodies influence the way in which we think. Lakoff and Johnson argue that "metaphor is not just a matter of language … on the contrary, human *thought processes* are largely metaphorical".[9] We associate 'up' with positive things and 'down' with negative things. We associate 'forward' with good things and 'backward' with bad things. Affection is warmth; anger is heat; love is an electric force. Even when we understand a new idea, we say "I see".

9   Lakoff and Johnson, *Metaphors We Live By*, p. 6.

Human beings think in metaphors – and many of these metaphors originate from the universal experience of occupying a human body.

You probably use bodily metaphors all the time in the classroom unconsciously. They are part and parcel of language and thought. Society, for instance, is often likened to a living body. A dictator might 'brainwash' his people. However, new body metaphors and analogies are easy to find and (relatively) simple to invent. It is also easy to encourage students to imagine their own bodies and perceptions as central when forming new understanding:

Let's imagine you were holding …

Think of what would happen to you if …

What would you see if …

The writer James Geary puts it perfectly: "Abstract concepts only take flight when tethered to the language of the body."[10]

Immediate environment

If you contextualise hypothetical scenarios within your shared environment, then they are easier to imagine. You could discuss how the classroom power dynamic might work differently if you were a *tyrannical* teacher. You could use the personal preferences of the students in the class to introduce the concept of percentage. You could introduce the grammatical term 'preposition' by helping students to see the physical relationships between objects – desks, chairs, the ceiling – in the classroom.

School environment and local context

Power hierarchies and spatial concepts can be taught in reference to staffing struc-tures and the organisation of school spaces. Like the tennis court example, places that all students use and visit regularly are excellent reference points. You could teach the notion of hyperinflation in reference to school canteen prices. You could

---

10 James Geary, *I is an Other: The Secret Life of Metaphor and How It Shapes the Way We See the World* [Kindle edn] (New York: HarperCollins, 2011), loc. 1887.

superimpose society onto your three-storey school building to introduce the concept of the British class system. Similarly, you could use analogies with local landmarks, local events and local celebrities beyond the school gates – assuming they are known by all students.

Shared cultural references

Cultural references from beyond the immediate vicinity of the school and local area come with a health warning. If you like to pepper your lessons with cute *Star Wars* allusions, witty football jokes or even political references then you are likely to alienate at least some of your students. That is not to say that your lessons should be mundane and drained of personality; just that you could fall victim once again to the dreaded 'curse of knowledge' if you try to use such allusions as purposeful teaching tools. The comparison may seem obvious to you, but it won't be to everyone.

The challenging concepts you are teaching become all the more challenging for a child if they have to learn the entire defensive line-up of your favourite football team alongside the intricacies of rock formation! Besides, many of your students will come from homes where English is the second language, and many will have had differing formative cultural and religious experiences. Part of the challenge of pedagogy is helping students with diverse home lives and backgrounds to each find meaning in the curriculum. However, once you get to know your classes well, you can begin to relate to personal interests at an individual level.

Please note that I am not suggesting that wider cultural references have no part to play in the classroom. Of course they do. Instead, I am arguing that they are sometimes unreliable in helping all students to make an initial connection with new material.

Distinct metaphors

The more distinct and unique – or even unusual – a metaphor, the less likely it is to become confused with a similar idea or be forgotten. In a sense, a metaphor can also be seen as a memory device – a mnemonic. Cognitive psychologist Daniel Willingham points to the way in which indistinct cues are a major cause of forgetting:

> **Some to-be-remembered material interferes with other to-be-remembered material, and the greater the similarity between them, the more likely that the cues will be the same, and therefore the more ambiguous they will be.**[11]

This highlights one of the dangers of the overuse of metaphors involving the immediate environment. If, for instance, the school building has been likened by different teachers not only to the class system, but also to the food chain and sedimentary layers of rock, it is very possible that these ideas will become entangled and, as Willingham suggests, ambiguous. It is important, therefore, to spend time sharpening your analogies and to adapt them if you notice that ideas are getting muddled.

---

11 Daniel T. Willingham, Ask the Cognitive Scientist: What Will Improve a Student's Memory?, *American Educator* (winter 2008–2009): 17–25, 44, at 19. Available at: https://www.aft.org/sites/default/files/periodicals/willingham_0.pdf.

Non-analogies are also very useful in helping students to map the boundaries of an idea. The act of comparing and contrasting similar ideas helps to provide clarity and accuracy. For instance:

> Was Hitler the same kind of tyrant as Stalin?

> Did J. B. Priestley and John Steinbeck share the same political beliefs?

> Does human skin work in the same way as the surface of a leaf?

Be careful though. If students' knowledge of the source (the first item studied) is insecure, you might unwittingly be helping them to create ambiguous cues.

Visual metaphors

"The soul never thinks without a picture." These words, attributed to Aristotle, remain a potent reminder of the power of images, and, as we know from Chapter 3, the simultaneous presentation of words and images is beneficial for learning. For now, we should note that people usually rate metaphors with vivid and concrete imagery as being the most memorable.[12] When I was studying A level English literature, I remember reading *Wuthering Heights* and struggling with the concept of a 'frame narrative'. I understood how it worked in Brontë's novel, but I struggled to put it into words. Nevertheless, once I had made a connection with Russian dolls I never looked back. A frame narrative is a story within a story (and sometimes within another story ...). The simple and elegant image of the Russian dolls was very effective in unlocking my understanding of this literary technique.

When possible, it is best to present metaphors and analogies through words *and* visuals – though time constraints mean that this is not always possible. This can help a child with a foundational knowledge gap to quickly catch up with their peers. Not everybody knows what a Russian doll is, for instance, but a quick picture would solve that problem straight away.

---

12 See Geary, *I is an Other*, loc. 839.

A geography teacher might open their teaching of the earth's layers by drawing an association with a hard-boiled egg:

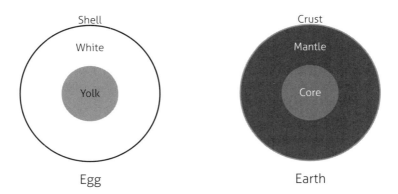

The crust is brittle and broken into pieces, like the cracked shell of a hard-boiled egg. The mantle is like the egg white, the core is like the yolk in the centre. This simple visual cue is distinct, relevant and potentially transformational. Terra firma seems a little less firm when you think of it as being as fragile as an eggshell! Metaphors like this are so effective because they allow us to 'see' what is not visible. In this case, the seemingly unknowable depths of the earth beneath our feet.

The double-edged sword

At some point, all analogies break down and fail. Cells live, whereas Lego is plastic and non-living. Tennis courts are two-dimensional, unlike three-dimensional atoms. The centre of a hard-boiled egg does not imitate the solidity of the earth's inner core. The simple sources and analogues we have used in this chapter belie the complexity of the targets on which they aim to shed light. More worryingly, Harrison and Treagust, whose research has involved the observation of the use of analogy in science teaching, state that "when students are left to interpret analogies on their own, they can just as easily construct alternative conceptions as the desired scientific conception".[13] Unfortunately, analogies can cause misconceptions as well as generate learning.

Harrison and Treagust recommend the three-step FAR guide for the systematic teaching of analogies: focus, action, reflection.[14]

1   **Focus** involves a consideration of the difficulty of the concept, students' prior knowledge of it and the familiar experiences that can be used to develop an analogue (the source of an analogy).

2   **Action** begins by checking that students are familiar with the analogue – for example, a hard-boiled egg. It then moves on to discussing how the analogue is like and unlike the target – for example, how is the egg like the earth? And how is the egg unlike the earth?

3   **Reflection** involves considering whether the analogy was clear or confusing, and planning changes for the next lesson and the next time the analogy is taught.

Ultimately, Harrison and Treagust suggest that analogies are very useful tools that can enhance teaching, but only when used carefully. Interestingly, they note that an analogy does not "provide learners with all facets of the target concept and that multiple analogies can better achieve this goal".[15] However, they also point out that some students struggle with multiple explanations and will favour a single representation of a phenomenon, even if it does not capture the concept in its entirety.

---

13 Allan G. Harrison and David F. Treagust, Teaching and Learning with Analogies: Friend or Foe?, in Peter J. Aubusson et al. (eds), *Metaphor and Analogy in Science Education* (Dordrecht: Springer, 2006), pp. 11–24 at p. 20. Available at: https://pdfs.semanticscholar.org/8518/367cc1ef090ea263c39e912a4acaf59dd3d5.pdf.

14 Harrison and Treagust, Teaching and Learning with Analogies, p. 20.

15 Harrison and Treagust, Teaching and Learning with Analogies, p. 22.

The role of the subject curriculum

A rich, sequential and coherent subject curriculum provides students with a ready-built system of connections. As we know, cognitive science shows us that we learn in the context of what we already know. Daniel Willingham suggests that teachers should first ask: "What do students already know that will be a toehold on understanding this new material?"[16] A meticulously planned curriculum – from key stage to key stage, year to year, term to term, and topic to topic – gives teachers and students a familiar language and knowledge base with which to create these toeholds. This is even more powerful when the curriculum is designed in a way that encourages durable long-term learning – perhaps through the use of spaced practice and retrieval practice techniques.[17]

Therefore, the most efficient, effective and powerful metaphors are those that allude to a shared and well-remembered past. "Remember when we studied that? This is going to be similar."

Chapter summary

- Metaphors and analogies provide a bridge between students' current knowledge and material to be learnt. They are especially useful when working with abstract concepts that have few obvious real-world referents.

- The most effective metaphors are transformative, relevant, distinct and visual. The source of a metaphor should usually be a social, physical or emotional experience that all children can relate to.

- Metaphors must be considered a starting point, not an end point. They should be deployed with care. If not, students may embed misconceptions.

16 Willingham, *Why Don't Students Like School?*, p. 210.
17 See John Dunlosky et al., Improving Students' Learning with Effective Learning Techniques: Promising Directions from Cognitive and Educational Psychology, *Psychological Science in the Public Interest* 14(1) (2013): 4–58. Available at: http://www.indiana.edu/~pcl/rgoldsto/courses/dunloskyimprovinglearning.pdf for more.

First steps

- Make a conscious note of the metaphors and analogies that you use in lessons over the next few days. Which seem most successful? Which are less successful? Why do you think this is so? Becoming conscious of how you already use metaphor and analogy is your first step.

- Work with colleagues to begin compiling a list of effective metaphors and analogies in your subject area. A Google search or a question posed on Twitter can also provide rich pickings.

- If you are a subject or school leader, make metaphor and analogy collection and sharing a key part of your CPD work.

Chapter 6
Storytelling

Your students are pre-wired to learn from storytelling.

For countless years, I have enjoyed teaching the work of the First World War poet Wilfred Owen, whose lines have etched a hellish vision of trench warfare into the world's consciousness. It is hard to find anyone who is not moved in some way by Owen's writing. My lessons would always begin with a brief overview of Owen's biography accompanied by a very basic bullet-pointed slide show:

Wilfred Owen, 1893–1918
- Enlisted in the army in 1915.
- Left for the western front early in 1917.
- Diagnosed with shell shock and sent to Craiglockhart War Hospital, where he met Siegfried Sassoon.

- Returned to France in August 1918 and in October was awarded the Military Cross for bravery.
- On 4 November 1918 he was killed while attempting to lead his men across the Sambre canal at Ors. The news of his death reached his parents on 11 November, Armistice Day.

My fairly disinterested class would talk hear me talk through these facts one by one before we moved on to the true business of the lesson: the poetry. And so, for many years, my Wilfred Owen lessons began in exactly this way. *Click on the slide. Explain.*

Unbeknown to me, however, something far more stirring and human was afoot in the classroom next door. I discovered this when I popped my head in one day. My colleague, the young whippersnapper Russ Shoebridge, was also telling Wilfred Owen's life story. But in his classroom he was doing just that: *telling it* as a story and evoking an emotional response.[1]

I'd like to tell you about Wilfred Owen and this story epitomises the tragedy that was the pointless loss of innocent lives during the First World War.

Now Wilfred Owen was a patriot who was passionate about defending his country. Maybe you would be the same. Maybe we'd all be the same in the face of war.

---

1 Reproduced with Russ' permission – see Andy Tharby, Using Storytelling as an Explanation Tool, *Class Teaching* [blog] (7 July 2017). Available at: https://classteaching.wordpress.com/2017/07/07/using-storytelling-as-an-explanation-tool/ for more.

Now, Owen didn't join the war until 1915 ... and the first year for him seemed to be ... new and exciting!

Then, in January 1917, Wilfred Owen had his first experience of the front line ... and it would never be the same again.

After just a year on the front line, he had suffered concussion, he'd been gassed, he'd been evacuated with shell shock.

At this time, from the front line, he began to produce a series of his more famous poems, one of which we're going to read later on in the lesson today ...

Some people believe that Wilfred Owen didn't actually face any rifle fire until one week before the end of the war.

On 11 November 1918, the day that the war ended, as the bells were ringing out for peace in Wilfred Owen's home village in Shropshire, his parents received the telegram to inform them that, seven days ago, their son had been shot and killed on the bank of a river in northern France ...

In Russ' classroom, the students were leaning in to hear more, shocked and mes-merised in equal measure. After a short, stunned silence, a few hands went up from students who wanted to clarify the tragic irony of Owen's death in their own words. Russ' room was a far cry from the empty boredom of next door where my class were twiddling their pens or trying to catch the eye of the person behind them. And this gigantic difference in response was caused by just one thing: the fact that Russ had shared Owen's life as a story, not as a list of atomised facts.

Take a look back at how Russ so skilfully constructed his tale. At first he provided a cue that a story was about to start: "I'd like to tell you about ..." Next, he positioned his students in the story: "Maybe you would be the same." Following this, he provided a hint of the learning that was to come: "one of which we're going to read later on in the lesson today". And, finally, his short tale rounded off with the full tragic force of the protagonist's death: "his parents received the telegram to inform them that, seven days ago, their son had been shot and killed on the bank of a river in northern France ..." A further subtlety lay in the way that Russ' story neatly introduced the conflict inherent in Owen's work: the idealistic image of brave, heroic soldiers against the realism of the brutality and emotional trauma of the battlefield. What a way to start a lesson!

In recent years, storytelling in the classroom has become a dying art. Too often, more attention is paid to the structure of the lesson and the sequence of activities than to the inherent emotional structure of the material itself – its human narrative. This is not only a shame but also a terrible oversight. As we will see as this chapter unfolds, a well-told story not only injects energy and empathy into a room, but will also improve every part of the learning experience, including later retention.

Stories make us human

To fully understand how the human brain became so primed to learn from the medium of storytelling, we must take a journey back through the mists of time to the origin of modern *Homo sapiens*. About 100,000 years ago, human cognitive abilities – learning, remembering and communicating – were far more limited than they are today. At some point between 30,000 and 70,000 years ago an extraordinary change took place. Human beings developed the capacity to communicate and share knowledge through remarkably subtle language exchanges. It seems that language and storytelling evolved hand in hand.

There are two prevalent theories about how human language might have developed. The writer Yuval Noah Harari refers to these as "the gossip theory and the there-is-a-lion-near-the-river theory".[2] Storytelling is at the heart of both theories. The first theory refers to the complexity of relationships in human societies. Gossiping was vital to the success of early hunter-gatherer bands. For a human society to successfully survive and reproduce, its members would need to keep track of constantly changing alliances and allegiances – who dislikes whom, who to trust, who to avoid and who has been invested with power. It's no wonder that modern teenagers – descendants, not to forget, of these first humans – are so obsessed with social media: it's gossip on tap! The second theory refers to the way in which stories were used to warn others of, and protect them from, imminent danger – in this case, the hungry lion down by the river. Over time, human societies

----

2 Yuval Noah Harari, *Sapiens: A Brief History of Humankind* (London: Harvill Secker, 2014), p. 27.

became united through ever more sophisticated and complex stories: the great binding myths of religion and nationhood, for example.

Fast-forward through time to our contemporary age and our genetic legacy has a profound influence on the workings of the modern human brain. Psychologists now tell us that stories are "psychologically privileged".[3] In other words, your students are pre-wired to learn from storytelling.

What makes stories so effective?

Evidence from the field of cognitive science tells us that storytelling has three important benefits for teachers and their students. Stories are *interesting*, they are *easy to understand* and they are *easy to remember*.[4]

1   **Stories are interesting** not only because they focus on themes that we can all relate to, but because they are not too hard and not too easy. They provide us with puzzles and questions and, it would appear, we tend to find the process of solving these interesting.

---

3   Willingham, *Why Don't Students Like School?*, p. 66.
4   See Daniel T. Willingham, Ask the Cognitive Scientist: The Privileged Status of Story, *American Educator* (2004): 43–45, 51–53. Available at: https://www.aft.org/periodical/american-educator/summer-2004/ask-cognitive-scientist.

2   **Stories are easy to understand** because we intrinsically know the structure and patterns of a story. We know that events and characters are causally related to each other, we know that there will be obstacles along the way and we expect that the ending will provide us with some new insight.

3   **Stories are easy to remember** because they provide a web of interconnecting and causally related parts. We remember an important event, which leads us to remember a main character, which leads us to remember their motive, which reminds us of another event ... Descriptive and explanatory formats, which tend to have fewer related parts, make the retrieval process much harder.

In *Made to Stick*, the writers Chip and Dan Heath explore how stories are put to use in the business and advertising worlds:

> The story's power, then, is twofold: It provides simulation (knowledge about how to act) and inspiration (motivation to act). Note that both benefits, simulation and inspiration, are geared to generating *action*.[5]

Brain scans reveal that when we imagine something – whether it's a flashing light or someone tapping on our skin – the same areas of the brain are activated as would be by the real physical event.[6] The sensations are *simulated* in the brain. Stories also provide *inspiration*: when you hear about how someone you can identify with has found unexpected success or has defeated a familiar demon, you begin to become convinced that you too might be able to do something similar.

This is what stories can do in the classroom: they help students to visualise *what* is possible, and they also map out *how* this can be made possible. It is no surprise that successful, vibrant and confident schools are those that overflow with stories.

Broadly speaking, there are three ways in which stories can be used to enhance learning. The first is to design complete lessons as if they were stories. The second is to use features of storytelling within your standard lesson format. And the third is to simply tell more stories. For the remainder of the chapter, we will explore a

5   Chip Heath and Dan Heath, *Made to Stick: Why Some Ideas Take Hold and Others Come Unstuck* (London: Arrow Books, 2008), p. 206.
6   Mark R. Dadds et al., Imagery in Human Classical Conditioning, *Psychological Bulletin* 122(1) (1997): 89–103.

number of tricks and slights of hand that all teachers, irrespective of stage or subject, can put to use immediately.

Rising and falling fortunes

Telling stories of past students – their successes and setbacks – is one of the most effective ways to enrich your lessons. Such stories are so useful because your students can easily identify with the protagonist – *he sat in this classroom, in that seat over there, wearing the same uniform as you.* These stories are usually used for one of two purposes: to inspire emulation, or to warn against a certain course of action – the time-honoured cautionary tale. As such, stories can be used for both motivational and instructional purposes.

For readers unfamiliar with narrative theory, most specialists agree that all stories conform to one of a few elementary shapes or emotional trajectories; however, there is disagreement as to the exact categorisation and definition of these. In 2016, a team of researchers analysed 1,737 stories from Project Gutenberg's fiction collection and found what they describe as "six core emotional arcs" that involve a rise and/or fall in fortunes. These are:

1. "Rags to riches" (rise).

2. "Tragedy", or "Riches to rags" (fall).

3. "Man in a hole" (fall–rise).

4. "Icarus" (rise–fall).

5. "Cinderella" (rise–fall–rise).

6. "Oedipus" (fall–rise–fall).[7]

These structures probably feel familiar. As a species, we have long relied on these shared patterns of narrative to define our existence. Interestingly, the most popular story arcs among readers – measured by number of downloads – are the

7   Andrew J. Reagan et al., The Emotional Arcs of Stories Are Dominated by Six Basic Shapes, *EPJ Data Science* 5 (2016): 1–8, S1–15 at 6. Available at: https://arxiv.org/pdf/1606.07772v2.pdf.

Cinderella and the Oedipus, along with two sequential man in a hole arcs (fall–rise–fall–rise) and Cinderella with a tragic ending (rise–fall–rise–fall).

This finding is not just an interesting curiosity; these same stories tell and retell themselves in your classroom. You just have to know where to look. For example:

Background	Story arc	Story
Sam, a student in your Year 9 English class, is despondent after receiving a low grade on an essay she wrote as an end of year assessment. Sam is a talented writer but the issue was that she did not support her points with relevant examples from the text.	"Man in a hole" (fall–rise)	You tell Sam the story of Megan, a student you taught three years ago. Megan was having the same problem as Sam when she was in Year 9 – her ideas were not rooted in textual evidence. Megan decided that every time she began an analytical essay she would write PEE (point, evidence, explain) in the margin and she would limit herself to half a side of writing per point to curb her tendency to digress. This strategy was so successful that Megan eventually achieved the highest possible grade – a 9 – in her English GCSE and is now pursuing the subject at A level.

Your Year 11 class have done especially well in their recent mock exam; their results were a vast improvement on a similar test the class had taken six months before. You are worried that a few members of the class are likely to become complacent.	"Oedipus" (fall–rise–fall)	You tell the story of Jake, a student you taught last year. He struggled with maths in Year 9, made considerable improvement in Year 10, but made the foolish decision to spend very little time revising for his final GCSE as over-confidence got the better of him. He is now in Year 12 and preparing to resit his GCSE exams.

These examples reveal how stories of former students can be used both to instruct and to motivate. The first example shows the great power of attaching a story to a metacognitive strategy: not only does Sam now have clarity about what she needs to do to structure a supported paragraph, but she can also visualise the kind of success she could achieve if she follows the advice. The second example is a classic cautionary tale. The truth is that we are motivated by risk avoidance as much as, if not more than, we are by visualising future success.

If you are a new teacher without a library of stories about previous students to fall back on, you could use anecdotes from your own school days or, failing that, you could always make them up.

The human element

Every school subject is a story in itself. As we explored in Chapter 1, over hundreds or even thousands of years, each subject has carved out its own shared imaginative space and specialised language domain through the combined effort and ingenuity of countless individuals, some of whom have even risked their lives or their freedom in the pursuit of truth. School subjects, even the sciences, are not objective truths; they have come to exist because of the value that human societies place on them. Subject disciplines are not static relics from the past: they continue to evolve because they are the result of continued human endeavour.

One of the causes of disaffection – in students and teachers – is the perception that the material being taught lacks relevance, which occurs when there appears to be very little relationship between the work students are completing and the very human history of the subject. Often tasks can feel irrelevant: why do I need to know how to calculate the circumference of a circle? The answer "because you need to be able to do this in the exam" is, of course, a reductionist cop-out. But what do we do about it?

One solution is to place the founding stories and characters of the subject in the foreground. Some teachers and schools are beginning to do just this. In these schools, maths facts are introduced with reference to Euclid's *Elements* and art lessons include the stories of the lives and times of great artists and art movements. Scratch the surface of any topic and there is a great wealth of character and emotion just waiting to be explored. Some of these stories are already well known – Isaac Newton and the falling apple, for instance. But there are vast treasure troves lying undiscovered in the hinterland of each subject, just waiting to be explored.

One trumps one million

The great power of a story – fact or fiction – lies in the emotional impact it has on the receiver. Usually, this is caused by the way in which the reader or listener is able to empathise with, or relate to, a character. Over the centuries, stories of individual people in extraordinary situations have captured the public imagination. Through their bravery, their suffering or their unexpected leadership, these ordinary people have become *cause célèbres* whose actions have changed the course of history. Think of the stoicism and courage of Rosa Parks or of the suffering of Phan Thi Kim Phuc, the 9-year-old Vietnamese victim of US napalm bombing, the photo of whom led to the public realisation and condemnation of the atrocities committed in the Vietnam War.

Stories are extremely useful when we want our students to care about the material they are learning or the messages we are communicating. The Heath brothers refer to what they call the 'Mother Teresa principle' – *if I look at one, I will act.* They point to the finding that statistics and figures often evince a purely analytical response in the receiver, whereas stories about individuals cause an emotional reaction.[8] Even if it feels counterintuitive, you are more likely to pull on your students' heart-strings if you tell them a tragic story about a child suffering during the Irish Potato Famine than if you share the horrifying statistics. The one, it seems, trumps the one million.

Conflict and anticipation

Stories hinge on conflicts and tensions which, in turn, create obstacles to be dodged and problems to be solved. The conflict in Shakespeare's *Romeo and Juliet*, for example, is set up when the scions of rival families flout social expectation and fall passionately in love. For the remainder of the play, our hearts are in our mouths: will their fragile love survive? Can they escape the twin evils of family expectation and fate?

---

8   Heath and Heath, *Made to Stick*, pp. 165–167.

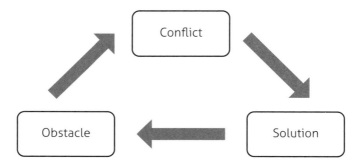

The history of knowledge is the history of resolved conflicts – until, of course, a new obstacle comes along to disrupt the equilibrium. Lessons can be set up in this way, where one question leads to another in a domino effect of causal exploration.

This is an iterative process that can be used either as a structure for delivering a lecture-style presentation or as a way of guiding a more interactive class investigation. One of my favourite examples of this structure in action comes from a TED Talk by the astronomer Natasha Hurley-Walker called 'How Radio Telescopes Show Us Unseen Galaxies', which is carefully structured around a series of problem and solution pairs that guide her audience through the history of telescope design:[9]

Problem 1: the universe is too vast to view.

Solution 1: the advent of the telescope.

Problem 2: the visible spectrum only shows a tiny slice of the known universe because everything appears red.

Solution 2: radio astronomy means that we can peer more deeply into the known universe.

Problem 3: radio waves have low resolution.

Solution 3: build huge radio telescopes in flat, dry, radio-quiet locations.

9   Natasha Hurley-Walker, How Radio Telescopes Show Us Unseen Galaxies, *TEDxPerth* [video] (18 April 2017). Available at: https://www.ted.com/talks/natasha_hurley_walker_how_radio_telescopes_show_us_unseen_galaxies.

Problem 4: these are still not sensitive enough to pick up very low and faint frequencies.

Solution 4: build a radio telescope one thousand times bigger and more sensitive that may allow us to watch the beginning of time itself.

A problem–solution structure not only gives complex material an internal structure, but also allows teachers to build up anticipation and intrigue; each problem acting as a primer for the next solution.

Storytelling and metacognition

According to a guidance report by the Education Endowment Foundation (EEF), metacognition is defined as:

> pupils' ability to monitor, direct, and review their learning. Effective metacognitive strategies get learners to think about their own learning more explicitly, usually by teaching them to set goals, and monitor and evaluate their own academic progress.[10]

The report recommends seven methods for improving students' metacognitive skills, which include:

- Explicitly teach pupils *metacognitive strategies*, including how to plan, monitor and evaluate their learning.
- *Model your own thinking* to help pupils develop their metacognitive and cognitive skills.
- Explicitly teach pupils *how to organise*, and effectively manage, their learning independently.

10 Alex Quigley et al., *Metacognition and Self-Regulated Learning: A Guidance Report* (London: Education Endowment Foundation, 2018). Available at: https://educationendowmentfoundation.org.uk/public/files/Publications/Campaigns/Metacognition/EEF_Metacognition_and_self-regulated_learning.pdf.

All three of these approaches can be enhanced by using stories as memorable examples or by adopting a narrative style. Indeed, the whole process of planning, monitoring and evaluating is a story in itself – with a beginning, a middle and an end. For instance, you might teach your class how to organise their learning independently by setting up a hypothetical scenario:

> **Muhammad was desperate to revise for his GCSE mathematics exam. As soon as he got home, he grabbed his revision guide from the top of a pile, sat down in the living room and started to read through the notes on the laws of indices. He found it hard but he persisted. Soon, his brother arrived home and turned on the television. Muhammad divided the next two hours between reading through his revision guide and watching children's TV shows.**

At this point, you can guide your students towards what Muhammad should have done. Hint: follow a revision plan; test himself with flashcards rather than reading notes; find a quiet place to revise; set reasonable short-term revision goals; and have appropriate breaks.

In another context, the storytelling device is useful for when we are modelling metacognitive processes:

The first time I tried this problem I made the mistake of ...

Last year, one of my students tried ...

Don't make the same mistake as Muhammad last year – he ...

When I first looked at this problem I didn't know where to start. And then it hit me that I should ...

It's okay to feel frustrated at this point. I often do. Now the best way to ...

Sometimes the advice we are given about how to improve our teaching feels abstract and hard to connect with – especially in the case of metacognition, which must win the award for the slipperiest term in education. However, once you start picturing abstract ideas as stories, exploring them in your classroom becomes a lot more manageable.

Starts and ends

All writers, poets and storytellers are acutely aware of the importance of beginnings and endings. The opening to a story either entices or repels us, while the ending – Will they? Won't they? Who did it? – is the destination we eagerly anticipate. When you think of your favourite novel or film, you probably recall with ease the events of its opening sequences and its closing moments. This phenomenon also appears in the classroom: people are more likely to remember the first and last part of an explanation of a new topic or procedure. These symmetrical effects are known by psychologists as the 'primacy effect' and the 'recency effect'. When information is presented in a sequence, most people remember what comes first and what comes last, but not the bit in between – the perfectly named 'hole-in-the-middle effect'.[11] However, once we start to gain expertise in an area, these effects become reduced.

How, then, do we capitalise on the primary and recency effects, but also soften the impact of the hole-in-the-middle effect?

● **Open with aplomb.** When introducing a new topic, we should 'frontload' crucial concepts, vocabulary and facts by drawing students' attention to their importance. The most straightforward way to do this is to get into the habit of using the phrase: "The most important thing about today's lesson/this

11 See Hattie and Yates, *Visible Learning*, p. 89.

topic will be ..." to introduce your through-line. Similarly, when modelling a new procedure – be it solving an equation or bowling a cricket ball – we should prime students to watch out for the main move: "While I do this, pay attention to the way that I ..."

- **Save the best for last.** Similarly, when you finish explaining, repeat the core message and have students repeat it back to you. The more times a student hears this message – or, even better, thinks about it – the more likely they are to remember it.

- **Illuminate the centre.** Take heed that your students are likely to forget the 'middle part' of an explanation, particularly when they are learning a demanding procedure or sequence of information. Find ways of making these hazy central sections more salient and distinct, perhaps with visual images, acronyms, striking metaphors, worked examples or old-fashioned repetition. For example, in mathematics, if you are giving students a series of five steps to solve an equation, be mindful that they are more likely to forget steps 3 and 4 than steps 1 and 5. In my lessons on Charles Dickens' *A Christmas Carol* (which is divided into five 'staves') I have noticed that my students are more likely to forget the events from stave 4 than any of the others. To counteract this, I now dedicate more classroom time to teaching and revising this stave.

Word biographies

Etymology is the study of the origins of words and the way in which their meanings have changed throughout history. Take the word 'etymology' itself as an example. The first part of the word 'etymo' derives from the Greek word 'etumos', meaning 'true'; the second part 'logy' derives from the Greek 'logos', which means 'the study of'. Therefore, etymology means 'the study of the origin (true meaning) of words'.

The hidden history of a word opens a gateway to its modern meaning. This can be combined with an appreciation of morphology, which is the study of the shape and form of words – or how the different parts of words are combined to make meaning. A simple way in which every teacher can tap into the power of stories is to introduce each new vocabulary term with its own mini-biography or an explanation of how the parts of the word combine to form its meaning. Not only will this make the word easier to understand and more memorable, it will also help to improve what Alex Quigley calls 'word consciousness', which is your students' curiosity about words and their meanings.[12]

An understanding of how prefixes work in the English language can be a good place to start. Here are a handful of the most common:[13]

Prefix	Meaning	Examples
anti-	against/opposed to	*anti-government, anti-aging, antisocial*
auto-	self	*automatic, autobiography, autodidact*
dis-	reverse or remove	*disagree, disown, disqualify*
hyper-	over	*hyperactive, hyperbole*
inter-	between/among/together	*interdependent, international*
mega-	very big, important	*megabyte, megawatt, megalomania*
post-	after	*post-war, postmodernism, postnatal*
pre-	before	*prehistoric, predestination, prefabrication*
tele-	at a distance	*television, telekinetic, telemarketing*

The trick is to provide a two-minute detour into the origin of a new word at the moment you introduce it, especially if it has an interesting or memorable back-story. This is a simple strategy with huge implications for the development of students' subject and vocabulary knowledge.

....

12 Alex Quigley, *Closing the Vocabulary Gap* (Abingdon and New York: Routledge, 2018), p. 19.
13 Online dictionaries and etymology guides, including https://www.etymonline.com/, are brilliant for sourcing word biographies.

The curriculum as a story

It is not just the lesson that should be thought of as a story, it is the curriculum itself. Imagine a five-year curriculum that hangs together like a nineteenth-century Russian novel: grand, sweeping themes; conflicting binary ideas (with several shades of grey in between); plots and subplots (and sub-subplots); lessons as chapters; and major thinkers as pivotal characters. Such a curriculum would be laid out sequentially but allow students to make new, insightful associations as their knowledge and understanding slowly accumulates. It would be polyphonic too, allowing room for dissident thinkers and alternative voices. Lessons would never feel stand-alone or atomised; instead, each would begin by picking up the thread of this overarching narrative that leads students by the hand into an intellectual alternative reality. The mind and memory are cultivated by stories, connections and associations – an ambitious, meticulously planned curriculum can provide this nourishment.

Even if you are a long way off such a curriculum, there are a few practical ways of bringing this utopian vision a little closer to reality:

- Begin each lesson with a review that links back to the previous lesson and beyond.

- End each lesson with a summary and a hint of what is to come.

- Continually make connections between topics – and encourage students to do this too.

- Use a visual map or timeline (even if you are not a geography or history teacher) and add to it each time you introduce a new topic. This way, your class have a unifying basis of understanding, to which they can link their ideas. For example, some art teachers plot their curriculum against a timeline that runs from the Ancient Egyptians to the postmodernists. Each time a new artist, style or movement is introduced to the class, this is added to the timeline so that students can begin to visualise the subject of art as an interweaving progression of methods and philosophies as well as a set of highly refined skills.

And finally, note that these ideas are not new. Here is Ted Clarke, the former head of chemistry at Porthcawl Community School:

> My main idea was to present science as a series of stories which were all linked together. Of course, the pupils may not understand some of the scientific words, so these would need to be explained using mini stories as well. The language used by teachers must vary depending upon the ability of the classes and the volume of the oral delivery must vary constantly as well.[14]

Beyond storytelling

A final word on storytelling. Even though storytelling is an excellent teaching and learning method, in most academic disciplines it is not the principal form of discourse. Teachers should make a clear distinction between the use of narrative devices in classroom talk and the expository or analytical nature of academic thought, speech and writing. If not, students may make the mistake of writing in a narrative style when this is not suitable. However, the story format comes with many natural benefits: it is memorable, exciting and nourishing. You should aim to make the most of it.

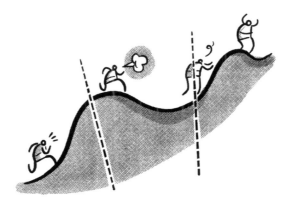

---

14 Quoted from the foreword to Shaun Allison, *Making Every Science Lesson Count: Six Principles to Support Great Science Teaching* (Carmarthen: Crown House Publishing, 2017), p. ii.

Chapter summary

- The human brain is primed to learn from stories. They are interesting, easy to understand and easy to remember.

- Teachers should tell stories about the rising and falling fortunes of former students; they should find the 'human element' of their subject; and they should base lessons around the central conflicts of the topic.

- To encourage deep and durable learning, a curriculum should be associative, cumulative and sequential. In essence, a five-year story.

First steps

- Read a non-fiction book for a lay audience on an aspect of your subject. These are often replete with excellent stories that can be lifted out and planted straight into your lessons.

- Look through the next scheme of work you will teach. Where are the central conflicts? How might you adapt your plans in light of these?

- Take a huge sheet of paper and map out your curriculum. Draw connections within and between topics. Consider how you would use these insights to enhance your provision.

Chapter 7

Elaboration

Explanations are only effective when students are also given the opportunity to think about the new material.

You have just finished explaining the causes of the Vietnam War to your Year 11 GCSE history class. You feel you have made a good job of it. You were careful not to overload working memory, you drew analogies to a previous topic on Nazi Germany and you used a map and a timeline as visual supports. Your class are now sitting quietly looking at you.

Finally you ask: "So, did you all understand?"

James, in the front row, didn't fully understand the causal connections you made in your explanation. However, James is a shy and polite boy; he respects you as a teacher and he really doesn't want to offend. James says nothing.

Sophie, who sits next to James, also found the explanation difficult to understand and would really like to let you know this. Nevertheless, she too says nothing. Like many teenagers, Sophie is acutely sensitive about losing face in

135

front of her peers; she would rather not understand than draw attention to herself in front of the whole class.

At the back sits Jake. He is swinging on his chair and inspecting his ink-splashed hands. He understood some of your explanation, but lost attention when his pen 'exploded' at about the time the French pulled out of Vietnam. Jake knows that he did not 'get' your explanation, but that does not matter to him. He has no interest in developing a deep understanding of a topic he finds, quite frankly, as dull as dishwater. He says nothing.

Over in the corner sits Anita. She listened intently throughout your explanation, alternating between nodding along and jotting down a few notes. Anita now feels that she knows the causes of the Vietnam War inside out and back to front. But unfortunately she doesn't. The problem is that she does not realise this. Like the others, Anita says nothing.

And finally, there's Leroy. Leroy understood everything straight away. In fact, if you asked him now he could repeat everything you said verbatim.

For the majority of this book, we have looked at how teachers design and deliver explanations; in this chapter, we shall turn our attention to students' reception of this new material. The scenario above demonstrates just how complex teaching can be: one explanation, five very different individual responses. Classroom power structures, peer culture, levels of motivation and 'illusions of knowledge' (when your understanding is more flimsy than you realise) all contribute towards the ways in which new material is received and responded to by your students. You might think, "Well, at least there's Leroy!" ... but you will need to think again. A further problem lies in memory retention. Will Leroy remember this new information in a week, a month or even a year? It's very possible that he will not. Genuine learning, of course, involves permanent changes to long-term memory.

Constructivist education theory concerns how individual people make sense of their surroundings. In recent years, it has been criticised by some as promoting student-centred, minimal-guidance teaching methods that have at their core the discredited idea that knowledge can simply be discovered by novice learners (see Chapter 3). However, the traditional notion that knowledge is neatly photocopied from the teacher's mind to the student's is also way off the mark.

Constructivist theorist Keith S. Taber argues that the truth is somewhat different:

> Each learner develops personal knowledge that is a unique reconstruction of the teacher's knowledge, by interpreting the public representation of the teacher's knowledge through available interpretative resources.[1]

In other words, a child's learning is always an interpretation of the teacher's explanation, and this is always constructed in light of their pre-existing mental schemas – their organised frameworks of prior knowledge – of the topic.

What kinds of explanations, then, are most likely to be effective? Two researchers from the University of Freiburg, Germany, Jörg Wittwer and Alexander Renkl, have proposed a four-part framework for understanding the effectiveness of instructional explanations:[2]

1   **They should be adapted to what the learner already knows.** Too hard and a breakdown of comprehension becomes likely. Too easy and the explanation will direct students away from learning more elaborate material.

1   Keith S. Taber, Constructivism as Educational Theory: Contingency in Learning, and Optimally Guided Instruction, in Jaleh Hassaskhah (ed.), *Educational Theory* (Hauppauge, NY: Nova Science Publishers, 2011), pp. 39–61 at p. 44.
2   Wittwer and Renkl, Why Instructional Explanations Often Do Not Work.

2   **They should focus on concepts and principles.** As discussed in Chapter 4, deep conceptual knowledge is a prerequisite for solving novel problems and generalising across contexts.

3   **They should be integrated into ongoing cognitive activities.** Students should be compelled to engage with or apply the new material in follow-up activities. This way, they can make stronger connections with prior knowledge.

4   **They should not replace knowledge-construction activities.** When students have a reasonable level of prior knowledge, explanations can be less effective than knowledge-generation tasks – particularly if learners do not realise that they also need to meaningfully engage with the material.

This has two important implications for teachers and curriculum designers. The first is that teacher explanation should always be followed by a task that involves thinking about and elaborating on the new material. The second is that sometimes an explanation will not be the most effective course of action; when their prior knowledge is strong, students should generate learning themselves through elaboration tasks.

It is important to repeat a key message: this book does not argue that lecturing is an effective teaching technique. Explanations are only effective when students are also given the opportunity to *think about* the new material. This is not to say that, at times, all teachers may need to resort to a lecture-style delivery. For instance, you might find yourself taking over a new class who have not been taught a significant percentage of the curriculum despite the fact that an important national assessment is looming. In this situation, you may have no choice but to limit the time your class has to interact with the new material in order to get through the content, in the hope that at least some of the material will stick.

For the rest of this chapter, we will explore how you can hand over responsibility for explanation to your students in a structured, scaffolded and evidence-informed way. The strategies and ideas that follow will help you to assess your students – to find out what they know and understand – and improve the chance that the material will be easy to retrieve from memory in the future. Most important, they provide the chance for students to construct well-developed mental models – or schemas – of the knowledge that you have carefully introduced in your explanation.

Ask questions

Let's return to the history lesson on the Vietnam War and what we could have done differently. The biggest mistake was the question "So did you all understand?" While younger children are more likely to be open and honest, many teenagers struggle to admit to a lack of understanding in public. We cannot ever know whether a student has understood something or not until we investigate more thoroughly. However you look at it, there is only one solution: the teacher needs to ask some questions.

There are no hard and fast rules for questioning, but planning your questions in advance is very sensible advice. Many expert teachers spend more time planning questions than anything else. They know that these will tease out how students are thinking and nurture new insights and connections. Be that as it may, skilful questioning involves adapting to the moment and developing new questions in response to the answers you receive. For this reason, listening very carefully to students' responses, and using these to create an accurate model of how they are thinking, is essential to effective questioning. This is a crucial element of your pedagogical content knowledge – your understanding of how students think about the topic and the possible misconceptions and misunderstandings that might be forming (see Chapter 1).

Over many years, a strong body of evidence has developed on effective questioning, which is summarised in the following table:[3]

Teachers need to ...	Why?
Ask some questions!	Teaching with questions is more effective than teaching without questions.
Avoid off-topic questions.	Questions should centre on the salient elements of the material to be learnt.
Use quick-fire factual questions.	When the material is factual, use lower-order questions and keep the pace of questioning brisk.
Match the level to the student.	As a rule of thumb, the majority of questions should be higher-order when teaching older and higher-ability students. Lower-order questions should be used the majority of the time with younger and lower-ability students.
Use wait time.	Give students time to think by leaving three seconds or more after posing a question. Leave longer for students to think about higher-order questions than lower-order questions.
Redirect and probe.	Move the questioning around the room to keep all students involved. Probe some students further to unpick their thinking.
Praise sparingly.	Avoid criticising student responses, but praise very sparingly. When using praise, make it very clear what you are praising. Avoid vague or unspecific comments.

3   See Kathleen Cotton, Close-Up #5 Classroom Questioning, *School Improvement Research Series* (1988). Available at: http://educationnorthwest.org/sites/default/files/ClassroomQuestioning.pdf.

Barak Rosenshine's review of studies into the most effective teachers adds four new insights:

1   The most effective teachers spend more than half of class time *lecturing, demonstrating* and *asking questions*; less effective teachers ask fewer questions.

2   They also ask a large number of students and *check the responses* of all students.

3   They ask students to *explain the processes* they use to find an answer; the least effective teachers ask almost no process questions.

4   They obtain a *high answer success rate* (about 82%) – suggesting that questions should not be too difficult, but not so easy that they provide no cognitive challenge.[4]

Finally, my favourite two pieces of questioning advice are:

1   **Surface to deep:** start with simple, surface questions to glean general understanding and to make key points salient. Then move to deeper questions that enable new insights and connections.

---

4   Rosenshine, Principles of Instruction, 17.

2   **Pan and probe:** get ideas from a range of students – from a variety of cognitive ability profiles – and then choose one or two individuals whose understanding will be probed in more depth.

Ask why

Elaborative interrogation is the act of creating new connections by linking unfamiliar material to existing knowledge. A fairly robust finding from education research is that getting students to answer why questions facilitates and improves learning. This is probably because these questions cause students to process material at a deeper level, or because such questions help students to better organise ideas in their minds.[5] Either way, elaborative interrogation is a simple strategy to put into practice.

It generally involves asking students to generate an explanation of a fact or idea that they have been learning about. Most studies have looked at the effects of the following four question types:[6]

5   Weinstein et al., Teaching the Science of Learning, p. 10.
6   Dunlosky et al., Improving Students' Learning, p. 8.

Why ...?

Why is this true?

Why does it make sense that ...?

Why would this fact be true of x and not of y?

The final question, which involves the act of comparison, has been shown to be the most effective of the lot – a good example of the power of teaching through contrasting examples. For example, you might ask, "Why is it colder in the winter than in the summer?" To answer this question, your students would then have to find the connection between the temperature and the season. The act of generating an explanation to answer this question, it would seem, will improve students' understanding of facts about the seasons.

Elaborative interrogation questions need not only be asked by teachers. Students also can be trained to generate their own elaboration questions. However, do remember that, first, students require a reasonable amount of prior knowledge for elaborative interrogation to work successfully. For example, if you are not a scientist, try answering this question: "Why is the theory of relativity true?" It is simply not possible without a huge amount of physics knowledge. Second, students will not always know where to direct elaborative questions. It may help to provide them with a list of facts or prompt material in advance for them to question.

Furthermore, teachers find why questions to have several other useful applications. First, they allow us to hear how students are reasoning and making inferences about a problem. Consequently, we can fill any knowledge gaps and nip potential misconceptions in the bud. Second, why questions encourage students to extend and develop their ideas, an essential habit required in extended academic writing. Finally, you can give students time to identify their knowledge gaps and areas of confusion and use these to devise their own why questions for you.

Explain it back

A worthwhile way of finding out how students have received and interpreted an explanation is to give them a short 'explain it back' task. These activities can take a range of forms, each with a slightly different purpose.

Explain it back to me

After talking through a concept, procedure or set of instructions, choose a student in the class to repeat each step back verbally. This gives you an immediate model of their thinking. Watch out for missing steps or steps placed in the wrong order. You will often find that students struggle to prioritise the key points and give greater weight to less-important information. This approach also gives students an extra incentive to listen: I must pay attention as it could be me who is called on to re-explain to the class.

Explain to your partner

Short paired tasks allow students to immediately practise with new material in their own words. They mean that everyone in the class gets the chance to put the newly taught material into action. Paired tasks work best when they are very tightly structured and clearly explained. For example:

"The person on the left has one minute to explain their understanding of cirrostratus clouds and how they are formed. The person on the right must listen in silence and then add anything they can. In a minute-and-a-half I will choose a pair to feed back to the class. Go."

During these conversations, your students may realise that there are some things about cirrostratus clouds that they do not fully understand. It feels safer to admit your knowledge gaps to the class as a pair than on your own. Another useful task, therefore, is to ask students to discuss and explain what they did not understand about a concept they have been taught. In truth, it is far more useful for the teacher to discover what has not been understood than what has. This works well as an end of lesson plenary task – it gives you something to review and fix at the start of the next lesson.

Write it down

A more academically rigorous approach is to have students write down what they have understood. Setting a word limit helps to keep the task very focused – for example, "Write down what we learn about Macbeth from the events of Act 2, Scene 2 in sixty words." This encourages prioritisation of the most important ideas. You can scaffold this task with a starter sentence: "In Act 2, Scene 2, we learn that Macbeth has become …" Or by providing students with a few key words to use in their answer.

Another version of this strategy involves displaying and explaining a slide or page of information, taking it away and then giving the class a short amount of time to write down as much as they can remember. This activates the 'testing effect', which will be discussed in this chapter.

Concept and fact checkers

Another useful way of immediately checking student understanding is to have the class complete a five-minute concept and fact checker. This is a quick list of short-answer or multiple-choice questions that allow a teacher to check the scope and depth of understanding. They are employed immediately after an oral or written explanation and completed on paper or on mini-whiteboards. These should not be confused with laborious comprehension questions: concept checks are sharp and brisk – taking no more than five minutes – and should always be followed by immediate feedback and discussion. During feedback, students should be encouraged to fill in the answers to any questions they skipped or elaborate on underdeveloped answers.

Here is an example of a fact checker that a science teacher could use after introducing students to the main features of stars. It is a very quick way to provide formative assessment. Students can self-mark or peer-mark, and teachers immediately find out what they need to reteach or where they need to elaborate further.

What is the closest star to earth?

Which two gases are stars mostly made from?

What holds a star together?

What is happening in the centre of a star?

According to star formation theory, where are stars 'born'?

When did stars start forming?

Write down two ways in which a star is different from a planet.

Peer tutoring

This is another approach that appears to have a positive impact on learning, according to the EEF's analysis. Peer tutoring involves children working in pairs and small groups and explicitly teaching each other. It appears to have benefits for students of all abilities and the EEF even found evidence that it has the greatest impact on low-attaining students and those from disadvantaged backgrounds. It works best when it is highly structured, when pairings and groupings are carefully thought through and when supports – such as questions and task lists – are provided. There is also a lot of evidence, again summarised by the EEF, to suggest that it is as beneficial (if not more so) to the tutoring student as it is to the tutee. Therefore, you should try to find opportunities for your lower-attaining students to act as tutors – perhaps to each other or to younger students. Despite the potential of peer tutoring, the EEF are at pains to point out:

Peer tutoring appears to be less effective when the approach replaces normal teaching, rather than supplementing or enhancing it, suggesting that peer

tutoring is most effectively used to consolidate learning, rather than to intro-duce new material.[7]

Retrieval practice (the testing effect)

You have explained a new concept with wonderful clarity. Every example, every anecdote, every analogy has hit the mark. Your students' new-found understand-ing is faultless. You finish the lesson proud of what you have managed to achieve. You move on to your next lesson still basking in the warm glow of success ... But a month later, when you set the same class an unexpected test on that material, the results are appalling: they have hardly remembered a thing.

A little-understood phenomenon in teaching is the fact that immediate perfor-mance is not a reliable measure of learning.[8] Instead, learning is a slow and iterative process and only truly occurs when there has been a permanent change to memory. As we explored in Chapter 3, learning involves the transfer of new material from the working memory to the long-term memory, where it needs to be encoded and stored. However, storing a new idea is not enough on its own; we also need to be able to retrieve it with ease whenever we require it. If sufficient time is not set aside for students to return to the content they have been taught and to practise recalling it from memory, then they are likely to forget it. This, then, begs the question of whether it was worth putting all the heartache into explaining the material in the first place.

That's why retrieval practice is explanation's best friend. It is probably the most effective way to combat the memory drainage problem. In simple terms, retrieval practice involves using a cue – usually a question – to test previously covered material. The act of dredging up knowledge from memory, or *retrieving* it, increases the likelihood that it will be remembered next time, and the harder it is to recall this knowledge, the more powerful the effect. Testing, therefore, not only shows what a student knows at a given point in time but also increases the likelihood that

---

7   See the EEF research summary: https://educationendowmentfoundation.org.uk/evidence-summaries/teaching-learning-toolkit/peer-tutoring/.
8   Nicholas C. Soderstrom and Robert A. Bjork, Learning versus Performance, *Oxford Bibliographies*. Available at: http://www.oxfordbibliographies.com/view/document/obo-9780199828340/obo-9780199828340-0081.xml.

the material will be remembered later. Studies also show that the best way to revise is to repeatedly test yourself; it is a far more powerful method than reread-ing or restudying the material.[9] Quizzing, multiple-choice questions and flashcards are all effective forms of retrieval practice.

Retrieval practice is most effective when utilised to complement the spacing effect – the finding that students are more likely to retain information if they keep coming back to it in increasingly spaced intervals.[10] This goes back to the nineteenth-century German psychologist Hermann Ebbinghaus, who first conducted research to identify the trend known as the 'forgetting curve', which shows how quickly new material is forgotten if it is not reviewed and practised at regular intervals.

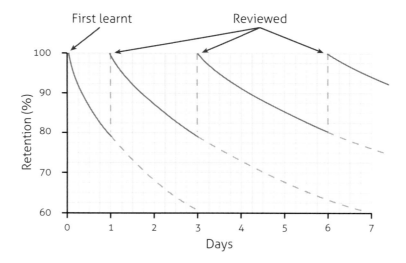

Retrieval practice is beneficial whenever you use it. It can form the basis of class-work or homework, can be initiated by the teacher or the students, and can be put to use at any point in a lesson. It works especially well as a regular starter activity. A rule of thumb might be to save the plenary of the current lesson for the start of

9   Henry L. Roediger and Jeffrey D. Karpicke, Test-Enhanced Learning: Taking Memory Tests Improves Long-Term Retention, *Psychological Science* 17(3) (2006): 249–255. Available at: https://www.ncbi.nlm.nih.gov/pubmed/16507066.
10 For a discussion on practical ways to combine retrieval practice and spaced practice see: Peter C. Brown et al., *Make It Stick: The Science of Successful Learning* (Cambridge, MA: Harvard University Press, 2014).

the next lesson. This allows time for forgetting and therefore enhances the power of the testing effect.[11]

Here is an example of a simple retrieval quiz I have used as a starter with my GCSE English literature classes when studying Ted Hughes' poem 'Bayonet Charge':

1. What was the soldier doing just before the poem started?

2. Which 'r' word is repeated in the first and second lines?

3. What is coming from "a green hedge"?

4. What simile is used to describe the rifle he is lugging?

5. Which 'p' word is used to describe the tear that he once had?

6. What does he almost do?

7. What is he said to be running like?

8. What simile is used to describe his foot?

9. What creature brings him back to reality?

10. What are this animal's mouth and eyes doing?

11. Which four items drop from his mind?

12. What does he want to escape from?

13. Write down three words to describe the feelings and emotions of the soldier.

The students complete the quiz individually and in silence. They are not permitted to check their notes – otherwise they would not be retrieving from memory. I reveal the questions one by one as this seems to increase attention and pace, and the quiz is followed by immediate feedback and self-marking. Finally, we discuss the hard questions and I ask why questions to develop students' thinking.

To reiterate, regular retrieval practice is the perfect companion to explanation. Retrieval practice has also been shown to identify gaps in knowledge, produce better organisation of knowledge, improve transfer of knowledge to new contexts

11 See Allison and Tharby, *Making Every Lesson Count* for a more detailed discussion.

and encourage students to keep studying.[12] It is the gift that keeps on giving. In fact, it can solve many problems and make up for a lot of unexceptional teaching. Because, let's face it, no teacher explanation is ever perfect.

The classroom as a dialogue

Robin Alexander's work on dialogic teaching marks a fascinating and energising way to end this chapter. Over the last few decades, Alexander's work has sought to make sense of observational data from classrooms around the world. Dialogic teaching is a pedagogical approach that centres on successful and meaningful classroom talk and aims to offer an alternative to the restrictive and traditional initiation–response–evaluation (IRE) exchange structure which involves closed questions, single-word answers, little elaboration and very basic feedback.[13] The dialogic approach has at its heart the relationship between student talk and teacher talk. Alexander considers the way in which classroom interactions can open up students' speaking and listening skills and, in turn, their thinking. He writes that "it is largely through the teacher's talk that the student's talk is facilitated, mediated, probed and extended – or, all too often, inhibited".[14]

In a dialogic classroom, talk is collective, reciprocal, supportive, cumulative and purposeful. In other words, the students learn together by listening, sharing ideas and expressing ideas freely, building on and connecting to each other's contributions – all in the direction of a clear learning goal.[15]

Alexander names sixty-one indicators that you might use to specify in practical terms what dialogic teaching comprises. These include:

- Questions that cause further thinking.

- Answers that are built upon by others.

---

12 Henry L. Roediger et al., Ten Benefits of Testing and Their Applications to Educational Practice, in Jose P. Mestre and Brian H. Ross (eds), *The Psychology of Learning and Motivation, Vol. 55: Cognition in Education* (San Diego, CA: Elsevier Academic Press, 2011), pp. 1–36.
13 A recent EEF trial found some promising evidence of the effect of dialogic teaching, see: https://educationendowmentfoundation.org.uk/projects-and-evaluation/projects/dialogic-teaching#closeSignup.
14 Robin Alexander, Developing Dialogue: Process, Trial, Outcomes, paper delivered at the 17th Biennial EARLI Conference, Tampere, Finland (31 August 2017). Available at: http://www.robinalexander.org.uk/wp-content/uploads/2017/08/EARLI-2017-paper-170825.pdf, p. 2.
15 Alexander, Developing Dialogue, p. 5.

- Exchanges that 'chain together'.

- Discussion that challenges thinking.

- Scaffolding of 'linguistic tools' to help students to access new understanding.

An interesting inclusion is "professional mastery of subject matter which is of the depth necessary to liberate classroom talk from the safe and conventional".[16] Once again, a teacher's pedagogical content knowledge is a prerequisite for enabling challenging and inspiring talk and thought in the classroom.

Alexander's description of the dialogic classroom is a utopian vision. From my experience, it is much easier to facilitate this kind of classroom talk when working with high-attaining or highly motivated students than it is when working with low-attaining or disaffected students. Unfortunately, these ideas can also be mis-interpreted to mean 'get in groups and have a chat about it' in the hope that children will, through some ethereal inner magic, come up with wonderful ideas all by themselves. Even though these practices might feel democratic and inclusive, they can have a hugely damaging effect on those children who do not have the prior knowledge, motivation or social skills to take part effectively.

Perhaps dialogic teaching should instead be considered a desirable outcome. Through the thorough and agile explanation of facts, concepts and procedures, students can build enough competence and expertise to participate in a supportive and challenging dialogue that promotes further insights and connections.

16 Alexander, Developing Dialogue, p. 10.

Thinking makes it so

There is no simple answer to the question "Who should speak more, the teacher or the student?" The answer is always contingent on whether the class have enough knowledge and understanding to do so effectively or not.

In *Why Don't Students Like School?*, Daniel Willingham wrote the simple, elegant sentence, "Memory is the residue of thought."[17] It is a powerful mantra, and reminds us that explanation must also cause students to think. If it does not, they are unlikely to learn anything from it.

Chapter summary

- An explanation should always be followed by, or broken up by, an activity that causes students to elaborate on and think about the new material. This will support the construction of new knowledge schemas.

- Regular retrieval practice tasks should be built into lessons and the curriculum so that students are able to retain the knowledge they have been taught.

- Dialogic teaching is a noble aim. It involves the facilitation, probing and extension of student talk through a shared dialogue.

First steps

- Aim to ask a why question at least three times in your next lesson.

17 Willingham, *Why Don't Students Like School?*, p. 54.

- Choose one class and use a retrieval practice quiz at the start of every lesson for the next half term. Keep a watch out for the effect this has on knowledge retention.

- Get into the habit of extending students' verbal answers by using just one question: "Can you develop that point?"

Conclusion: Getting better at explaining

There's only one corner of the universe you can be certain of improving, and that's your own self.

Aldous Huxley[1]

In this book, we have pared down the concept of explanation into a set of interrelated principles, strategies and classroom tools. In this conclusion, we will look at the skill of explaining in the same way as we might consider the development of expertise when learning the violin or how to play netball.

Research into expertise draws a clear line between the way in which experts and novices solve problems.[2] Whereas novices are likely to have fragmented and disconnected knowledge of a 'domain' (in our case, classroom explanation), experts have developed extensive, deep and well-organised mental representations. In practice, this means that problem-solving becomes effortless and automatic for experts. An expert explainer has many tricks at their fingertips; they can adapt their talk to fit the student and situation by choosing from a repertoire of flexible,

1 Aldous Huxley, *Time Must Have a Stop* (London: Vintage Classics, 2015 [1944]).
2 K. Anders Ericsson and Robert Pool, *Peak: Secrets from the New Science of Expertise* (New York: Houghton Mifflin Harcourt, 2016).

well-honed strategies. This occurs with very little conscious thought at all. To the outside observer, they appear to be a natural.

This, however, is an illusion. Classroom expertise is almost always hard-won, and sometimes is the result of years of failure and trial and error. I could advise you to go and watch someone who is very good at explaining. You might come away with a couple of useful ideas to transfer into your practice; however, this would not necessarily help you to understand the thought processes that reinforce a teacher's in-the-moment decisions. Watching another teacher is useful, but much remains hidden from you.

To develop the skill of explaining, we need to take heed of the research into how people use purposeful practice to develop their expertise in any skill domain.[3] Purposeful practice involves a repeating process:

- Setting a goal.

- Monitoring progress towards the goal.

- Seeking feedback.

- Resetting the goal.

The ideas in the final section of this conclusion will use this iterative sequence as a basis.

Before we explore that, there is a second problem to acknowledge: explaining is also subject and topic specific. An English teacher may have become very skilled at explaining Shakespeare's *Othello* but be less proficient at explaining *Hamlet*. This might be caused by the fact that they studied *Othello* at university or simply because they have just had more experience of teaching that play. As we explored in Chapter 2, this means two things. First, that content knowledge plays an important hand in the development of the skill of explanation. Second, that it is not always accurate to describe a teacher as good at explanation *per se*; expertise is influenced by the specific content to be taught – sometimes we know it, sometimes we don't.

All is not lost, however. As we have explored in this book, there are many generic skills and ways of thinking about explanation that transfer across subjects beautifully – awareness of the curse of knowledge, teaching in short bursts, combining

---

3   See Ericsson and Pool, *Peak* for a discussion of this.

words and images and using real-world examples, concrete analogies and story-telling devices to name a few. If we really want to improve the way in which we explain we should take a dual, overlapping approach: improve the generic skill of explanation and develop the richness of our content knowledge.

How to improve your teacher explanation

Set up your classroom strategically

There is a close relationship between the way in which you organise your class-room and the likelihood that your explanations will prove to be successful. Careful groundwork creates the climate and environment for active and fruitful listening. Consider implementing the following:

- **Reciprocal eye contact.** Desks and seating should be organised so that all students can see you; in fact, most students dislike it when their view is obstructed or uncomfortable. You can achieve this through arranging your classroom in traditional rows or horseshoes, or by reorganising the room during the explanation section of the lesson. During an explanation, the teacher should always remain the focal point.

- **Stand still.** Avoid the temptation to move around the room too much. This is distracting and requires students' extra effort to maintain attention. If you are presenting from the board, be sure to stand to the side of it and not obscure the view.

- **Find an explanation 'perch'.** Some teachers like to choose a particular place to stand or sit when giving an explanation. If you always use the same spot to deliver essential ideas and messages, your students will subconsciously invest this location with importance.

- **Seating plans.** Experienced teachers know very well that there is an art to creating a successful seating plan, one that is borne out of a heady mix of design and evolution. A great seating plan will ensure that: easily distracted students are kept apart; those with hearing and visual impairments can see and hear your explanations; those who require extra one-to-one explanations are easy to reach; and that pairs are supportive and fill each other's gaps in understanding. It is amazing how many seemingly intractable problems can be cured by a simple seat change!

Teach listening skills

Too often, explanations fail to hit the mark because students are not listening properly. It is best to teach listening skills explicitly and to insist that listening protocols are followed to the letter. These might include:

- Look directly at the speaker.

- Stop working when the teacher is talking.

- Remain quiet when someone is speaking.

- Pay attention to the key point.

- Maintain an open posture to signal that you are paying attention.

- Ask questions – but only after the teacher has finished talking.

- Respect new ideas, even if you do not agree.

The time-honoured, oft-repeated golden rule for teachers is *never talk over the top of others*. Effort put into this at the start of the year always pays dividends by the end.

Script explanations

I would recommend that all new teachers spend some time scripting explanations, especially if the content is tricky. This allows you to prepare language and vocabulary choices carefully. In spoken language we typically choose less challenging vocabulary than we do when writing. Admittedly scripting can be very time-consuming, and so a quicker approach for more experienced teachers is to produce bullet-pointed paper notes or cue cards that can be referred to discreetly throughout the lesson. It is so easy to miss out steps or crucial information in the heat of the moment, so all teachers, even the most experienced, benefit from using pre-planned prompts, especially when teaching new material for the first time. Slide shows are also a possibility, but as we discussed in Chapter 4, detailed notes on slides are likely to overload your students' working memories and so become detrimental to learning.

A useful task is to write out an explanation and then rid yourself of superfluous examples or overcomplicated descriptions. Aim, always, for an economy of words. In time, good habits will become automatic and your spontaneous, responsive explanations are likely to improve too.

As we move through the key stages, textual explanations should start to replace spoken ones whenever possible. Alex Quigley explains why:

> No matter how well we model, scaffold and encourage academic talk in our classrooms, our talk simply won't prove as complex as the language of what our children read. Put simply, the older children become, the more how they talk becomes less like what they read.[4]

Rehearse explanations

This will help to ensure a fluent delivery. Consider the non-verbal elements of your explanation carefully as well. When will you modify your inflection to introduce excitement, suspense or place emphasis on a key point? When will you change the pace and volume of your talk? Where will you stand in the classroom? Will you use physical movement to indicate a change in topic or idea? What kind of gestures will you use to support meaning? When will you pause for dramatic effect or to allow thinking time? It is advisable, however, that you do not over-rehearse. It is best not to present yourself as robotic or inauthentic.

Observe explanations

If you are going to watch the explanations of other teachers, it is best to bring along an observation schedule like the one that follows. This will allow you to pinpoint their best moves and identify useful strategies to take back to your own classroom.

---

4   Quigley, *Closing the Vocabulary Gap*, p. 81.

Features	Frequency					Notes and examples
	Always	Usually	Sometimes	Once	Never	
Introduction is clear.						
Purpose of lesson is explained.						
Content is conceptual.						
Links are made to previous and/or future learning.						
New vocabulary is clarified through etymology/morphology.						
Key ideas are made salient and repeated.						
Language is combined with images.						
Short bursts of explanation are followed by practice.						

Features	Frequency					Notes and examples
	Always	Usually	Sometimes	Once	Never	
Parts of explanation are linked together.						
Attention is 'funnelled'.						
Real-world examples are used.						
Multiple examples are used.						
Non-examples are used.						
Concrete analogies are used.						
Misconceptions are highlighted and addressed.						
Features of storytelling are used.						

Features	Frequency					Notes and examples
	Always	Usually	Sometimes	Once	Never	
Students' grasp of main ideas is checked.						
Students elaborate.						
Retrieval practice is embedded.						
Students maintain attention.						
Changes to voice and gesture emphasise key points.						

You could also ask someone to observe you, using this schedule, or you could even film yourself and watch it back. When you require feedback on your explanation, it can be a good idea to ask a non-specialist to help – i.e. another teacher who does not teach your subject. They will be able to tell you whether your teaching is comprehensible to a novice.

Search for explanations

The task of self-generating explanations is extremely exhausting. There is no need to reinvent the wheel each time. Ask other teachers how they explain a topic or watch them in action – this creates a very specific focus for your observations. You can also search for examples, analogies and stories in books, articles, teacher blogs, textbooks, journals, TV documentaries and online lectures and talks. This will heighten your sensitivity to how speakers and writers capture difficult concepts with clarity and an economy of words. Teachers should work together to develop, test, refine and disseminate the best scripted explanations of difficult topics. It's an area in which we could really gain from pooling our expertise.

There is no need to be too precious about explanation. Remember that recorded and written explanations are also excellent ways of outsourcing or supporting explanations. As long as time is spent ensuring that students comprehend and elaborate on this new knowledge, multimedia resources are just as successful as teacher-led explanation.

How to help other teachers to develop their explanation skills

Place teacher talk at the centre of professional development

If you are a subject or school leader, teacher talk and explanation should be a key priority. You should do everything you can to demonstrate how much you value it. To create the kind of curriculum and learning opportunities that our students need, we must pay special attention to two essential questions: first, what should we teach and, second, how should we teach it? The truth is that nothing matters as much as this in a school. All opportunities to improve subject knowledge and explanation should be taken: in meetings, in INSETs and in those impromptu discussions at the photocopier. If you celebrate the ingenious ways in which the teachers you manage use words and language to breathe life into the curriculum, then you are likely to be nurturing a rich culture of academic learning.

Provide low-threat opportunities for teachers to watch each other

Create a climate where teachers feel comfortable to drop in to watch one another explain ideas. There are no perfect ways to teach each new concept or procedure, but some ways are more effective than others. Take the attention off an individual teacher's performance and consider instead the performance of the words they have employed. Remember that even the most experienced teacher can learn something fresh and interesting from listening to a rookie.

Make reading a CPD activity

Teachers should be encouraged to read books, articles and journals that support and enhance their teaching of the curriculum. Not only does this improve subject knowledge and provide explanation exemplars, but it also keeps them engaged and curious about their subject. I love nothing more than discovering something new about a topic I have taught several times before. You could do this via email or by popping an article in everyone's pigeon hole (if they still exist in your school!) or, even better, you could allocate regular meeting time to reading and reflection. If you are going to do this, make sure that you carefully facilitate the conversation so that teachers take away something concrete that they can use in their classroom.

Archive explanations

Keep topic-specific lists of useful misconceptions, examples, stories and scripted explanations. Supplement these with videos, lectures, talks and documentaries that add an extra layer of academic challenge to the curriculum. Update these regularly and use them to support the work of all teachers, especially your most inexperienced.

Prioritise the curriculum

Many of the chapters in this book have naturally gravitated towards the suggestion that schools and teachers should spend more time talking about the curriculum. Quite simply, the knowledge and skills that teachers explain in the classroom are always related to and associated with a wider network of these. The human mind consists of interconnected webs, and learning consists of slowly deepening understanding. If the curriculum is designed to mirror this, then students are likely to learn more and find lessons more interesting.

Model it yourself

Assemblies, whole-staff meetings, staff training and talks to parents are all examples of times when school leaders should model great explanation skills. These presentations should be well-structured, well-rehearsed and exhibit a degree of mastery over the main features of successful explanation. Public speaking may not be every senior leader's main strength – and nor should it be – but it is very difficult to expect teachers and students to sustain a culture of concise, elegant talk if it is not modelled by those who set the tone of the school. Clipped, jargon-heavy and business-like speech is acceptable – and sometimes even desirable – behind closed doors. But usually not in public. With a larger audience, slide shows should be direct, minimalist and uncluttered. Most importantly, a love of language and of knowledge should be implicit in every word spoken.

The aim of this book has been to promote a shift in your thinking about teacher talk and to give you manageable strategies to put into practice immediately. However, to bring about sustained change, you will need to integrate these ideas in small and deliberate steps.

It is frustrating, really, to think about how little time the teaching profession has dedicated to discussing and improving teacher explanation. It is hard to imagine academic and conceptual learning that has not originated from spoken, written or visual forms of exposition. And yet when you ask school leaders whether they have ever provided a training session on teacher explanation – as I have done – most will say that they have never thought to do this. More worrying is the fact that the opportunity to discuss how to teach subject-specific content effectively is also very rare. In the current climate, schools seem to prefer generic and controlling approaches to improving teaching and learning.

The implicit ideological opposition to teacher talk has left something of a black hole in teaching. For the sake of our students and our profession it is time to seize back our words, our language and our classrooms. If you are motivated to do anything after reading this book, then please start by raising awareness of the central role that teacher explanation should play in your school. It is time to start a conversation and, as with classroom dialogue, this is best initiated by those of us at the chalkface.

Thank you for reading.

Bibliography

Alexander, Robin (2017). Developing Dialogue: Process, Trial, Outcomes, paper delivered at the 17th Biennial EARLI Conference, Tampere, Finland (31 August). Available at: http://www.robinalexander.org.uk/wp-content/uploads/2017/08/EARLI-2017-paper-170825.pdf.

Allison, Shaun (2017). *Making Every Science Lesson Count: Six Principles to Support Great Science Teaching* (Carmarthen: Crown House Publishing).

Allison, Shaun (2017). Now That's What I Call CPD, *Class Teaching* [blog] (24 April). Available at: https://classteaching.wordpress.com/2017/04/24/now-thats-what-i-call-cpd/.

Allison, Shaun and Andy Tharby (2015). *Making Every Lesson Count: Six Principles to Support Great Teaching and Learning* (Carmarthen: Crown House Publishing).

Anderson, Chris (2016). *TED Talks: The Official TED Guide to Public Speaking* [Kindle edn] (New York: Houghton Mifflin Harcourt).

Aristotle (1991). *The Art of Rhetoric,* Hugh Lawson-Tancred (trs) (London: Penguin Classics).

Ayyildiz, Yildizay and Leman Tarhan (2013). Case Study Applications in Chemistry Lesson: Gases, Liquids, and Solids, *Chemistry Education Research and Practice* 14(4): 408–420.

Baddeley, Alan D. and Graham J. Hitch (1974). Working Memory. In Gordon H. Bower (ed.), *The Psychology of Learning and Motivation*, Vol. 8 (New York: Academic Press), pp. 47–89.

Barbash, Shepard (2012). *Clear Teaching: With Direct Instruction, Siegfried Engelmann Discovered a Better Way of Teaching* (Arlington, VA: Education Consumers Foundation).

Bauernschmidt, Althea (2017). Two Examples Are Better Than One, *The Learning Scientists* [blog] (30 May). Available at: http://www.learningscientists.org/blog/2017/5/30-1.

Beck, Isabel L., Margaret G. McKeown and Linda Kucan (2002). *Bringing Words to Life: Robust Vocabulary Instruction* (New York: Guilford Press).

Bernstein, Basil (1999). Vertical and Horizontal Discourse: An Essay, *British Journal of Sociology of Education* 20(2): 157–173.

Bettinger, Eric and Susanna Loeb (2017). Promises and Pitfalls of Online Education, *Evidence Speaks Reports* 2(15) (9 June). Available at: https://www.brookings.edu/research/promises-and-pitfalls-of-online-education/.

Blaich, Charles, Kathleen Wise, Ernest T. Pascarella and Josipa Roksa (2016). Instructional Clarity and Organization: It's Not New or Fancy, But It Matters, *Change: The Magazine of Higher Learning* 48(4): 6–13.

Brown, Peter C., Henry L. Roediger and Mark A. McDaniel (2014). *Make It Stick: The Science of Successful Learning* (Cambridge, MA: Harvard University Press).

Bryson, Bill (2016). *A Short History of Nearly Everything: A Journey through Space and Time* (London: Black Swan).

Camerer, Colin, George Loewenstein and Martin Weber (1989). The Curse of Knowledge in Economic Settings: An Experimental Analysis, *Journal of Political Economy* 97(5):

1232–1254. Available at: https://www.cmu.edu/dietrich/sds/docs/loewenstein/CurseknowledgeEconSet.pdf.

Centre for Education Statistics and Evaluation (2017). *Cognitive Load Theory: Research That Teachers Really Need to Understand* (September) (Sydney: NSW Department of Education). Available at: https://www.cese.nsw.gov.au//images/stories/PDF/cognitive-load-theory-VR_AA3.pdf.

Chandler, Paul and John Sweller (1992). The Split Attention Effect as a Factor in the Design of Instruction, *British Journal of Educational Psychology* 62(2): 233–246. Available at: https://onlinelibrary.wiley.com/doi/abs/10.1111/j.2044-8279.1992.tb01017.x.

Chen, Ouhao, Slava Kalyuga and John Sweller (2015). The Worked Example Effect, the Generation Effect, and Element Interactivity, *Journal of Educational Psychology* 107(3): 689–704.

Chinn, Clark A. and William F. Brewer (1993). The Role of Anomalous Data in Knowledge Acquisition: A Theoretical Framework and Implications for Science Instruction, *Review of Educational Research* 63(1): 1–49. Available at: http://journals.sagepub.com/doi/10.3102/00346543063001001.

Christodoulou, Daisy (2014). *Seven Myths About Education* (Abingdon: Routledge).

Christodoulou, Daisy (2016). *Making Good Progress? The Future of Assessment for Learning* (Oxford: Oxford University Press).

Clark, Richard E. (1982). Antagonism between Achievement and Enjoyment in ATI Studies, *Educational Psychologist* 17(2): 92–101.

Coe, Robert, Cesare Aloisi, Steve Higgins and Lee Elliott Major (2014). *What Makes Great Teaching? Review of the Underpinning Research*. (London: Sutton Trust). Available at: http://www.suttontrust.com/wp-content/uploads/2014/10/What-makes-great-teaching-FINAL-4.11.14.pdf.

Cordingley, Philippa, Toby Greany, Bart Crisp, Sarah Seleznyov, Megan Bradbury and Tom Perry (2018). *Developing Great Subject Teaching: Rapid Evidence Review of Subject-Specific Continuing Professional Development in the UK* (Coventry: CUREE). Available at: http://www.curee.co.uk/node/5032.

Cotton, Kathleen (1988). Close-Up #5 Classroom Questioning, *School Improvement Research Series*. Available at: http://educationnorthwest.org/sites/default/files/ClassroomQuestioning.pdf.

Cowan, Nelson (2010). The Magical Mystery Four: How is Working Memory Capacity Limited, and Why?, *Current Directions in Psychological Science* 19(1): 51–57.

Dadds, Mark R., Dana H. Bovbjerg, William H. Redd and Tim R. H. Cutmore (1997). Imagery in Human Classical Conditioning, *Psychological Bulletin* 122(1): 89–103.

de Bruyckere, Pedro, Paul A. Kirschner and Caspar D. Hulshof (2015). *Urban Myths About Learning and Education* [Kindle edn] (London: Academic Press).

Department for Education (2015). *Reading: The Next Steps: Supporting Higher Standards in Schools*. Ref: DFE-00094-2015 (London: Department for Education). Available at: https://www.gov.uk/government/uploads/system/uploads/attachment_data/file/409409/Reading_the_next_steps.pdf.

Derry, Jan (2013). *Vygotsky: Philosophy and Education* (Chichester: Wiley-Blackwell).

Dickens, Charles (1905 [1854]). *Hard Times* [Project Gutenberg ebook edition] (London: Chapman & Hall). Available at: https://www.gutenberg.org/files/786/786-h/786-h.htm.

Didau, David (2011). Zooming In and Out, *The Learning Spy* [blog] (11 July). Available at: http://www.learningspy.co.uk/english-gcse/zooming-in-and-out/.

Dobelli, Rolf (2013). The Overconfidence Effect: Why You Systematically Overestimate Your Knowledge and Abilities, *Psychology Today* [blog] (11 June). Available at: https://www.psychologytoday.com/gb/blog/the-art-thinking-clearly/201306/the-overconfidence-effect.

Dunlosky, John, Katherine A. Rawson, Elizabeth J. Marsh, Mitchell J. Nathan and Daniel T. Willingham (2013). Improving Students' Learning with Effective Learning Techniques: Promising Directions from Cognitive and Educational Psychology, *Psychological Science in the Public Interest* 14(1): 4–58. Available at: http://www.indiana.edu/~pcl/rgoldsto/courses/dunloskyimprovinglearning.pdf.

Ericsson, K. Anders and Robert Pool (2016). *Peak: Secrets from the New Science of Expertise* (New York: Houghton Mifflin Harcourt).

Evans, Darren (2012). Make Them Believe in You: Teacher Credibility is Vital to Learning, an Updated Study Reveals. But What Can You Do to Win Your Pupils Round?, *TES* (17 February). Available at: https://www.tes.com/news/make-them-believe-you-0.

Finn, Amber N., Paul Schrodt, Paul L. Witt, Nikki Elledge, Kodiane A. Jernberg and Lara M. Larson (2009). A Meta-Analytical Review of Teacher Credibility and Its Associations with Teacher Behaviors and Student Outcomes, *Communication Education* 58(4): 516–537.

Gathercole, Susan E. and Tracy Packiam Alloway (2007). *Understanding Working Memory: A Classroom Guide* (London: Harcourt Assessment).

Geary, James (2011). *I is an Other: The Secret Life of Metaphor and How It Shapes the Way We See the World* [Kindle edn] (New York: HarperCollins).

Gee, James Paul (1992). *The Social Mind: Language, Ideology and Social Practice* (New York: Greenwood Publishing Group).

Gee, James Paul (2011). *An Introduction to Discourse Analysis: Theory and Method* (Abingdon: Routledge).

Ginns, Paul (2005). Meta-Analysis of the Modality Effect, *Learning and Instruction* 15(4): 313–331.

Gorman, A. M. (1961). Recognition Memory for Nouns as a Function of Abstractedness and Frequency, *Journal of Experimental Psychology* 61: 23–39.

Haidt, Jonathan (2006). *The Happiness Hypothesis: Putting Ancient Wisdom to the Test of Modern Science* (London: Arrow Books).

Harari, Yuval Noah (2014). *Sapiens: A Brief History of Humankind* (London: Harvill Secker).

Harrison, Allan G. and David F. Treagust (2006). Teaching and Learning with Analogies: Friend or Foe?. In Peter J. Aubusson, Allan G. Harrison and Stephen Ritchie (eds), *Metaphor and Analogy in Science Education* (Dordrecht: Springer), pp. 11–24. Available at: https://pdfs.semanticscholar.org/8518/367cc1ef090ea263c39e912a4acaf59dd3d5.pdf.

Haskins, William A. (2000). Ethos and Pedagogical Communication: Suggestions for Enhancing Credibility in the Classroom, *Current Issues in Education* 3(4): 1–6.

Hattie, John and Gregory Yates (2014). *Visible Learning and the Science of How We Learn* (Abingdon: Routledge).

Heath, Chip and Dan Heath (2008). *Made to Stick: Why Some Ideas Take Hold and Others Come Unstuck* (London: Arrow Books).

Hurley-Walker, Natasha (2017). How Radio Telescopes Show Us Unseen Galaxies, *TEDxPerth* [video] (18 April). Available at: https://www.ted.com/talks/natasha_hurley_walker_how_radio_telescopes_show_us_unseen_galaxies.

Huxley, Aldous (2015 [1944]). *Time Must Have a Stop* (London: Vintage Classics).

Johnson, Zac D. and Sara LaBelle (2017). An Examination of Teacher Authenticity in the College Classroom, *Communication Education* 66(4): 423–439.

Kalyuga, Slava, Paul Ayres, Paul Chandler and John Sweller (2003). The Expertise Reversal Effect, *Educational Psychologist* 38(1): 23–31.

Kalyuga, Slava, Paul Chandler and John Sweller (1999). Managing Split-Attention and Redundancy in Multimedia Instruction, *Applied Cognitive Psychology* 13: 351–371. Available at: https://tecfa.unige.ch/tecfa/teaching/methodo/Kalyuga99.pdf.

Kind, Vanessa and Per Morten Kind (2011). Beginning to Teach Chemistry: How Personal and Academic Characteristics of Pre-Service Science Teachers Compare with Their Understandings of Basic Chemical Ideas, *International Journal of Science Education* 33(15): 2123–2158.

Kirschner, Paul A., John Sweller and Richard E. Clark (2006). Why Minimal Guidance During Instruction Does Not Work: An Analysis of the Failure of Constructivist, Discovery, Problem-Based, Experiential, and Inquiry-Based Teaching, *Educational Psychologist* 41(2): 75–86.

Kirschner, Paul A., John Sweller and Richard E. Clark (2012). Putting Students on the Path to Learning: The Case for Fully Guided Instruction, *American Educator* (spring): 6–11.

Lakoff, George and Mark Johnson (1980). *Metaphors We Live By* (London and Chicago: University of Chicago Press).

Leary, Timothy (2013). In Defense of Metaphors in Science Writing, *Scientific American* [blog] (9 July). Available at: https://blogs.scientificamerican.com/life-unbounded/in-defense-of-metaphors-in-science-writing/.

Leith, Sam (2012). *You Talkin' to Me? Rhetoric from Aristotle to Obama* (London: Profile Books).

Liu, Tzu-Chien, Yi-Chun Lin, Yuan Gao, Shih-Ching Yeh and Slava Kalyuga (2015). Does the Redundancy Effect Exist in Electronic Slideshow Assisted Lecturing?, *Computers and Education* 88: 303–314.

Lucariello, Joan and David Naff (n. d). How Do I Get My Students Over Their Alternative Conceptions (Misconceptions) for Learning?, *American Psychological Association* [blog]. Available at: http://www.apa.org/education/k12/misconceptions.aspx.

Marzano, Robert J. (2004). *Building Background Knowledge for Academic Achievement: Research on What Works in Schools* (Alexandria, VA: Association for Supervision and Curriculum Development).

Mayer, Richard E. (n.d.). The Five Principles [video]. Available at: https://www.kuleuven.be/english/education/educational-policy/limel/training-platform/script/the-cognitive-theory-of-multimedia-learning.

Mayer, Richard E. and Roxana Moreno (1998). A Split-Attention Effect in Multimedia Learning: Evidence for Dual Processing Systems in Working Memory, *Journal of Educational Psychology* 90(2): 312–320.

OECD (n.d.). *Country Note: England and Northern Ireland (UK): Survey of Adult Skills First Results.* Available at: http://www.oecd.org/skills/piaac/Country%20note%20-%20United%20Kingdom.pdf.

Paivio, Allan (1971). *Imagery and Verbal Processes* (New York: Holt, Rinehart and Winston).

Pinker, Steven (2014). *The Sense of Style: The Thinking Person's Guide to Writing in the 21st Century* (London: Penguin).

Pollock, Edwina, Paul A. Chandler and John Sweller (2002). Assimilating Complex Information, *Learning and Instruction* 12(1): 61–86.

Quigley, Alex (2018). *Closing the Vocabulary Gap* (Abingdon and New York: Routledge).

Quigley, Alex, Daniel Muijs and Eleanor Stringer (2018). *Metacognition and Self-Regulated Learning: A Guidance Report* (London: Education Endowment Foundation). Available at: https://educationendowmentfoundation.org.uk/public/files/Publications/Campaigns/Metacognition/EEF_Metacognition_and_self-regulated_learning.pdf.

Reagan, Andrew J., Lewis Mitchell, Dilan Kiley, Christopher M. Danforth and Peter Sheridan Dodds (2016). The Emotional Arcs of Stories Are Dominated by Six Basic Shapes, *EPJ Data Science* 5: 1–8, S1–15. Available at: https://arxiv.org/pdf/1606.07772v2.pdf.

Roediger, Henry L. and Jeffrey D. Karpicke (2006). Test-Enhanced Learning: Taking Memory Tests Improves Long-Term Retention, *Psychological Science* 17(3): 249–255. Available at: https://www.ncbi.nlm.nih.gov/pubmed/16507066.

Roediger, Henry L., Adam L. Putnam and Megan A. Smith (2011). Ten Benefits of Testing and Their Applications to Educational Practice. In Jose P. Mestre and Brian H. Ross (eds), *The Psychology of Learning and Motivation, Vol. 55: Cognition in Education* (San Diego, CA: Elsevier Academic Press), pp. 1–36.

Rosenshine, Barak (2012). Principles of Instruction: Research-Based Strategies That All Teachers Should Know, *American Educator* 36(1): 12–19, 39. Available at: https://www.aft.org/sites/default/files/periodicals/Rosenshine.pdf.

Rovelli, Carlo (2015). *Seven Brief Lessons on Physics*, Simon Carnell and Eric Segre (trs) (London: Penguin).

Schüler, Anne, Katharina Scheiter and Peter Gerjets (2013). Is Spoken Text Always Better? Investigating the Modality and Redundancy Effect with Longer Text Presentation, *Computers in Human Behaviour* 29(4): 1590–1601.

Shulman, Lee S. (1986). Those Who Understand: Knowledge Growth in Teaching, *Educational Researcher* 15(2): 4–14.

Standish, Alex and Alka Sehgal Cuthbert (2017). Disciplinary Knowledge and School Subjects. In Alex Standish and Alka Sehgal Cuthbert (eds), *What Should Schools Teach? Disciplines, Subjects and the Pursuit of Truth* (London: UCL Institute of Education), pp. 1–19.

Sweller, John (1994). Cognitive Load Theory, Learning Difficulty and Instructional Design, *Learning and Instruction* 4: 293–312. Available at: http://coral.ufsm.br/tielletcab/Apostilas/cognitive_load_theory_sweller.pdf.

Sweller, John (2006). The Worked Example Effect and Human Cognition, *Learning and Instruction* 16(2): 165–169.

Sweller, John, Jeroen J. G. van Merrienboer and Fred G. W. C. Paas (1998). Cognitive Architecture and Instructional Design, *Educational Psychology Review* 10(30): 251–298. Available at: http://www.csuchico.edu/~nschwartz//Sweller%20van%20Merrienboer%20and%20Pass%201998.pdf.

Taber, Keith S. (2011). Constructivism as Educational Theory: Contingency in Learning, and Optimally Guided Instruction. In Jaleh Hassaskhah (ed.), *Educational Theory* (Hauppauge, NY: Nova Science Publishers), pp. 39–61.

Teacher Development Trust (2015). *Developing Great Teaching: Lessons from the International Reviews into Effective Professional Development* (London: Teacher Development Trust). Available at: http://TDTrust.org/about/dgt.

Teven, Jason J. (2007). Teacher Caring and Classroom Behavior: Relationships with Student Affect and Perceptions of Teacher Competence and Trustworthiness, *Communication Quarterly* 55(4): 433–450.

Tharby, Andy (2017). Using Storytelling as an Explanation Tool, *Class Teaching* [blog] (7 July). Available at: https://classteaching.wordpress.com/2017/07/07/using-storytelling-as-an-explanation-tool/.

Titsworth, Scott, Joseph P. Mazer, Alan K. Goodboy, San Bolkan and Scott A. Myers (2015). Two Meta-Analyses Exploring the Relationship between Teacher Clarity and Student Learning, *Communication Education* 64(4): 385–418.

Twist, Liz, Juliet Sizmur, Shelley Bartlett and Laura Lynn (2012). *PIRLS 2011: Reading Achievement in England* (Slough: NFER). Available at: https://www.nfer.ac.uk/publications/PRTZ01/PRTZ01.pdf.

Waack, Sebastian (n.d.). Hattie Ranking: 252 Influences and Effect Sizes Related to Student Achievement, *Visible Learning*. Available at: https://visible-learning.org/hattie-ranking-influences-effect-sizes-learning-achievement/.

Weinstein, Yana, Christopher R. Madan and Megan A. Sumeracki (2018). Teaching the Science of Learning, *Cognitive Research: Principles and Implications* 3(2): 1–17. Available at: https://cognitiveresearchjournal.springeropen.com/articles/10.1186/s41235-017-0087-y.

Wiliam, Dylan (2011). *Embedded Formative Assessment* [Kindle edn] (Bloomington, IN: Solution Tree Press).

Willingham, Daniel T. (2004). Ask the Cognitive Scientist: The Privileged Status of Story, *American Educator*. 43–45, 51–53. Available at: https://www.aft.org/periodical/american-educator/summer-2004/ask-cognitive-scientist.

Willingham, Daniel T. (2006). How Knowledge Helps: It Speeds and Strengthens Reading Comprehension, Learning – and Thinking, *American Educator* 30(1): 30–37. Available at: https://www.aft.org/periodical/american-educator/spring-2006/how-knowledge-helps.

Willingham, Daniel T. (2008–2009). Ask the Cognitive Scientist: What Will Improve a Student's Memory?, *American Educator* (winter): 17–25, 44. Available at: https://www.aft.org/sites/default/files/periodicals/willingham_0.pdf.

Willingham, Daniel T. (2009). *Why Don't Students Like School? A Cognitive Scientist Answers Questions About How the Mind Works and What It Means for the Classroom* (San Francisco, CA: Jossey-Bass).

Wittwer, Jörg and Alexander Renkl (2008). Why Instructional Explanations Often Do Not Work: A Framework for Understanding the Effectiveness of Instructional Explanations, *Educational Psychologist* 43(1): 49–64.

Wragg, Edward C. and George Brown (1993). *Explaining* (Abingdon and New York: Routledge).

Young, Michael (2014). Knowledge, Curriculum and the Future School. In Michael Young, David Lambert, Carolyn Roberts and Michael Roberts (eds), *Knowledge and the Future School: Curriculum and Social Justice* (London: Bloomsbury), pp. 9–40.

Young, Michael (2014). Powerful Knowledge as a Curriculum Principle. In Michael Young, David Lambert, Carolyn Roberts and Michael Roberts (eds), *Knowledge and the Future School: Curriculum and Social Justice* (London: Bloomsbury), pp. 65–88.

Zohar, Anat and Simcha Aharon-Kravetsky (2005). Exploring the Effects of Cognitive Conflict and Direct Teaching for Students of Different Academic Levels, *Journal of Research in Science Teaching* 42(7): 829–855.

Making Every Lesson Count

Six principles to support great teaching and learning

Shaun Allison and Andy Tharby

Making
every lesson
count

Six principles to support great
teaching and learning

Shaun Allison and Andy Tharby
Foreword by Doug Lemov

978-184590973-4

This award-winning title has now inspired a whole series of books. Each of the books in the series are held together by six pedagogical principles – challenge, explanation, modelling, practice, feedback and questioning – and provide simple, realistic strategies that teachers can use to develop the teaching and learning in their classrooms.

A toolkit of techniques that teachers can use every lesson to make that lesson count. No gimmicky teaching – just high-impact and focused teaching that results in great learning, every lesson, every day.

Suitable for all teachers – including trainee teachers, NQTs and experienced teachers – who want quick and easy ways to enhance their practice.

ERA Educational Book Award winner 2016. Judges' comments: "A highly practical and interesting resource with loads of information and uses to support and inspire teachers of all levels of experience. An essential staffroom book."

Making every
English
lesson count

Six principles to support
great reading and writing

Andy Tharby

978-178583179-9

Making every
science
lesson count

Six principles to support
great science teaching

Shaun Allison

978-178583182-9

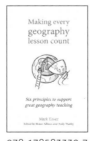

Making every
geography
lesson count

Six principles to support
great geography teaching

Mark Enser

978-178583339-7

Making every
history
lesson count

Six principles to support
great history teaching

Chris Runeckles

978-178583336-6

Making every
maths
lesson count

Six principles to support
great maths teaching

Emma McCrea

978-178583332-8